OUR *Ultimate* PURPOSE IN LIFE

The Grand Order of Design and the Human Condition

Hans-Juergen Strichow

BALBOA.
PRESS
A DIVISION OF HAY HOUSE

Balboa Press books may be ordered through booksellers or by contacting:

Balboa Press
A Division of Hay House
1663 Liberty Drive
Bloomington, IN 47403
www.balboapress.com.au
1 (877) 407-4847

Because of the dynamic nature of the Internet, any web addresses or links contained in this book may have changed since publication and may no longer be valid. The views expressed in this work are solely those of the author and do not necessarily reflect the views of the publisher, and the publisher hereby disclaims any responsibility for them.

The author of this book does not dispense medical advice or prescribe the use of any technique as a form of treatment for physical, emotional, or medical problems without the advice of a physician, either directly or indirectly. The intent of the author is only to offer information of a general nature to help you in your quest for emotional and spiritual well-being. In the event you use any of the information in this book for yourself, which is your constitutional right, the author and the publisher assume no responsibility for your actions.

Any people depicted in stock imagery provided by Thinkstock are models, and such images are being used for illustrative purposes only.
Certain stock imagery © Thinkstock.

Printed in the United States of America.

ISBN: 978-1-4525-1192-4 (sc)
ISBN: 978-1-4525-1193-1 (e)

Balboa Press rev. date: 10/28/2013

CONTENTS

PREFACE

"To be or not to be" is the famous opening phrase in William Shakespeare's play, where *'Hamlet'* questions the meaning of life, and whether or not it is worth to stay alive when life contains so many hardships.

As he concerns himself with the significance of life and existence in general, he comes to the conclusion that the main reason why people stay alive is due to a fear of death and the uncertainty of what lies beyond.

And whilst there have been a large number of proposed answers from many different cultural and ideological backgrounds and speculations throughout history, we are still largely in the dark and driven by fear.

The reason for this lies in part with the scientific community and its predominant focus on the empirical facts and figures about the physical nature of the universe and the parameters concerning the 'how' of life.

Yet, the answer is more so associated with the 'why' of life and the philosophical and religious conceptions of existence, social ties, consciousness, happiness, value, purpose and the conception of God.

An alternative approach poses the question "What is the meaning of 'my' life?" in which case the purpose of life may coincide with the achievement of an ultimate reality, a feeling of oneness, or even sacredness.

The truth of the matter appears to lie in a combination of both, whereby the human race is not just a collection of individuals pursuing their happiness in isolation, but a 'family of man' that is looking out for each other.

As it stands, this perception of reality has not yet filtered into the minds of the people around the world, the cause of which has to do with the absence of a common vision relating to 'Our Ultimate Purpose in Life'. (ref.: Appendix E)

Under the circumstances, anybody can claim a mandate, be it related to the individual's pursuit of its own happiness in isolation, with friends and family, the wider community, if not the entire human race.

This brings us to the proposition of a 'Grand Order of Design' and a sense of purpose relating to the 'how' and 'why' of our existence here on earth, as illustrated below under "Our Ultimate Purpose in Life".

Our Ultimate Purpose in Life

"To pursue the great unknown so as to advance the human race, using the process of trial and error.

As a consequence, many problems are caused by people; however they are also solved by people.

The degree of our problems at any one time is proportionate to the perception of reality by one and all".

Fig.: 0.1

As a consequence, the lower life forms do not have a problem with their perception of reality as their value system is entirely predetermined by the forces of Nature and the values manifested in the genes.

In contrast to the above, the growth and development of the human race is largely self-determined and aided by a culture reflecting the pursuit of the great unknown and trials and errors of our forefathers.

As it stands, our self-determination has led us to a point where the degree of our problems is proportionate to our lack of understanding with respect to 'who we are as an individual' and 'what we are doing on this planet'.

This brings us to the objective of this book/reference manual which is specifically aimed at:

a) The seekers of knowledge who are 'constructively discontent' with the scientific communities and/or belief systems and their answers to 'Our Ultimate Purpose in Life', which is leaving them in a moral vacuum.

b) The education, training and consulting facilities who are ultimately responsible for shaping the minds of the up and coming generations with respect to their desire and ability to create a better world for all mankind.

c) The businesses of industry which are left to the process of trial and error when it comes to their obligations as a human organization and commitment to the needs and expectations of the stakeholders, and vice versa.

As to aim c), the objective is based on a separate business manual reflecting my experiences and developments as a management consultant to the businesses of industry, as illustrated below under:

Part 3—The Human Organization:

3.1 Total Organization Performance

3.2 Human Resource Management

3.3 Human Resource Development

3.4 Business Process Management

3.5 Business Process Development

For further information, please contact hansstrichow@yahoo.com.au

The objective is aided and abetted by the use of pictures, models and graphs that are bound to be understood and remembered more so than the traditional volumes of words.

And whilst I have no qualms about my aspirations and desire to make the world a better place, I am equally aware of the fact that the future begins with us and our commitment to 'Our Ultimate Purpose in Life'.

In that context, we need to be familiar with "The History of 'The Meaning of Life' so far", as illustrated under Appendix A.

MY LIFE IN A NUTSHELL

I have just recently completed my autobiography, in which I refer to my life as being "all about fun, frustration and fulfilment", in that order, the latter of which is the reason for my writing this book/reference manual.

That is, after having successfully survived the rituals of life for seventy two years, I was compelled to consider my life experiences in the light of my fun, frustration, and potential fulfilment, or ultimate purpose in life.

As to the latter, I am not referring to my credentials as a scholar and achievements in any one of the sciences like Psychology, Psychiatry and similar established bodies of knowledge relating to 'The Human Condition'.

Instead, I am referring to my experiences as a seeker of knowledge relating to questions of "who we are as an individual, what we are doing on this planet, and where we are going as a human race", as you are about to find.

My desire to do so started many years ago in Germany when I was still a boy, who seemed to show signs of intelligence as my teacher suggested that I should embark on a higher education than was needed for a tradesman.

The option to become a tradesman was purely financial, as my parents were relatively poor and unable to support me that is, unless I was given a scholarship and prepared to work after school and thus pay for the cost of living.

This having been provided with the goodwill and support of my teacher, as well as my working as a caddy on the local golf course after school and during the weekend, I was now on my way to get an education.

And just when I was one year away from matriculating, my father decided to migrate to Australia in late 1959 as a complete family comprising an older sister, older brother, myself at 18 years old, and younger sister.

And so I started my new life in Melbourne as a process worker whilst I took classes in engineering and management after hours, which soon allowed me to prove myself in industry, where I quickly made a name for myself.

In the process, I became increasingly aware of the wasted potential, which bothered me to the point where I began to study the principles underlying "Human Resource Management" and "Business Process Management".

Having been there and done that, I wrote a series of manuals relating to the subject matter, which I then used to promote myself as a management consultant to the businesses of industry. (ref. Introduction)

This is when my fulfilment need came to the surface to the extent that I became obsessed with the principles underlying thought, conduct, knowledge, and the nature of the universe, which culminated in my writing this book.

At the same time, I was not satisfied with the mere concept of a book and the prospect of making some money, as I was hooked on the idea of providing a breakthrough in the way we were dealing with the problems of the world.

INTRODUCTION

Whilst I have focused my attention on the study and analysis of 'The Human Condition', I have extended my horizon to the universe as a whole in the belief that the two are intertwined within a 'Grand Order of Design'.

By 'The Human Condition' I am referring to *"The unique and inescapable features of being human, or the irreducible part of the human mind that is inherent and not dependent on factors such as gender, race or class".*

In doing so, I ended up deriving at an entirely new perception of reality with respect to the human mind and its ultimate purpose within the universal scheme of things, much of which is outside the proverbial square.

That is, according to the information stated in the Wikipedia and other recognized sources of information;

"The mind is the complex of cognitive faculties that enables consciousness, thinking, reasoning, perception and judgment—which may also apply to other life forms".

The main question regarding the mind is its relation to the physical brain and nervous system, where the mind is either separate from our physical brain or the same as the brain. (or some of its activities)

Another question is whether the mind is exclusive to human beings, possessed by some or all animals or by all living things, and whether the mind can also be a property of some types of man-made machines.

Whatever the case may be, it is generally agreed that the mind is that which enables a being to have subjective awareness and to perceive and respond to stimuli with a consciousness, thoughts and feelings.

The mind is understood in many ways by many different cultural and religious traditions, some of which see the mind as a property exclusive to humans, whereas others relate it to animals and to deities.

Some of the earliest recorded speculations have linked the mind (sometimes described as being identical with soul or spirit) to theories concerned with both life after death and cosmological and natural order.

This brings us to Albert Einstein who said that, *"The most incomprehensible thing about the universe is that it is comprehensible, whereby everything in the universe follows laws, without exception."*

Newton believed that *"Our habitable solar system did not arise out of chaos by the laws of nature, but that the universe was created by God at first and conserved by him to this day in the same state and condition."*

The idea arose because it is not only the peculiar characteristics of our solar system that seem oddly conducive to the development of human life, but also the characteristics of our entire universe—and its laws.

Even Aristotle believed in *'an intelligent natural world that functions according to some deliberate design or Science of God that is comprehensible like any other science relating to the body and the mind.*

By the same token, the science is not something that is to be believed in, but rather made known and measurable in the context of 'The Grand Order of Design', or 'GOD' for short, and 'The Human Condition'

And whilst we are studying the physical aspects of our body, the environment, and the universe, our understanding of our metaphysical dimension and purpose is still in its infancy, as we can see by the problems of the world.

The question is *"Does philosophy or the study of general and fundamental problems such as those connected with reality, existence, knowledge, values, reason, mind and language have the answers we need?"*

Given the fact that anyone can call themselves a philosopher and anything philosophical can be claimed to be the truth and no one can proof that the author is wrong, the answers may not come from this area.

And so I stopped calling myself a philosopher as I focused my attention on the connection between "The Grand Order of Design" and 'The Human Condition', as illustrated below.

The Grand Order of Design

```
                          |
        ┌─────────────────┴─────────────────┐
   The Laws of Physics              The Laws of Metaphysics
        (Nature)                          (Nurture)
     How we Survive                      Why we Live
        └─────────────────┬─────────────────┘
                          |
                     Principles
                          |
                     Practices
                          |
                The Human Condition
```

Fig.: 0.2

The illustration is portraying the laws of physics and metaphysics, whereby the principles and practices represent 'Our Ultimate Purpose in Life' or pursuit of the great unknown so as to advance the human race.

This brings me to the pseudo sciences or claims, beliefs and practices which are presented as scientific, but lack supporting evidence or plausibility, the reality of which is simply a part of 'The Human Condition'.

As a consequence, we have a responsibility as part of 'Our Ultimate Purpose in Life' to convert the pseudo sciences into known and measurable principles of life, or discard them as a misperception of reality.

In doing so, the proven principles of life must be tailored to suit the average person without a need for a university degree or similar qualification, as this would affect their acceptance by the community at large.

PART 1.0

THE GRAND ORDER OF DESIGN

1.1   The Forces of Nature & Nurture

When we look at the complexity of life, we can only come to the conclusion that life is the result of a meaningful relationship between a metaphysical intelligence and the physical building blocks of life.

After all, the building blocks like the atoms did not form themselves into the interdependent structures of this world from the algae and the single-celled animals to the businesses of industry and government.

By the same token, the structures did not equip themselves with a nervous system, the purpose of which was to report any life-threatening events to whom, the king building block or its representatives?

This brings us to the twenty amino acids and their role as a building block of proteins and as an intermediate in metabolism, which is determined by the sequence of the bases in the gene that encodes that protein.

The proteins not only catalyse all (or most) of the reactions in living cells, but they also control virtually all cellular processes, the nature of which remains one of the great unsolved mysteries of life.

Given the amino acids have led to the evolution of life culminating in the emergence of the human species, we are now facing an even greater mystery relating to our existence here on earth and in the universe.

In order to unravel the mystery, let us begin with our feelings relating to the adequacy of our basic needs and the fairness of our interaction needs, as illustrated below under "The Forces of Nature & Nurture".

The Forces of Nature & Nurture

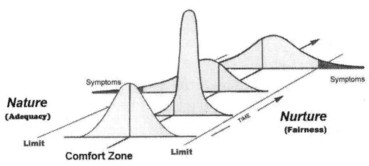

Fig.: 1.1.1

The illustration is portraying the natural or bell shaped distribution of our behaviour relating to a known comfort zone, which is not only different for every mind and body, but also constantly changing.

We can compare the phenomenon to our daily commuting and fitness of our body and mind, whereby our comfort zone is represented by the space between the white lines on the road to a given destination.

Under the circumstances, if we drive in the United Kingdom, the left line may represent the adequacy of our basic needs and the forces of Nature, and the right line the fairness of our interaction needs and the forces of Nurture.

In that context, it may be perfectly acceptable to drive all over the road and at any speed and condition of vehicle roadworthiness, simply because this is deemed fair to one and all, despite the associated losses of life.

On the other hand, the actual position on the road, the speed, the vehicle condition, the registration, the driver condition and numerous other factors may have become part of our laws and been deemed unfair by some.

And whilst we may be relatively clear with respect to the ultimate purpose of our wanting to use the car in the first place, the same cannot be said for the journey of life and our destination after our death.

This brings us to the space between the white lines, which is designed to accommodate the factors relating to the adequacy of our basic needs and the fairness of our interaction needs, or other road users, whereby:

The initial cost and ongoing maintenance of the road system is paid for by the community, regardless of whether or not we have a car and/or other means of transport, how much and how careful we drive, and so on.

The forces of Nature can now be addressed with respect to the priority factors like the adequacy of the vehicle and road surface etc., which can then be modified to reduce the financial burden to the community at large.

And whilst the adequacy requirements are relatively easy to deal with, the element of fairness represents a much more difficult situation, the cause of which lies in the perception of reality by one and all.

In either case, the timely modification of the root causes is bound to require a commitment of money, time and effort, which can always be delayed until the 'The Cost of Commuting' becomes a political football.

The scenario is only too familiar when it comes to our pressures in life and 'The Cost of Living' in general, which is an indication of 'Our Ultimate Purpose in Life', and the process of trial and error in particular.

One way of reducing the cost would be to reduce the distance between the white lines and to impose fines whenever the car is going outside the limits, in the hope that the drivers will adjust to the new measures.

If so, the new roads could be made narrower from thereon and thus save a lot of money, but there is only so much we can gain from this type of 'enforced change' before we reach the limits of our bodies and minds.

Another way would be to impose restrictions on our driving habits and to issue heavy fines whenever we fail to meet the specified limits, in which case we are also bound to increase the number of 'criminals'.

In the process, we may even become dependent on the steady flow of penalties or revenue, which is now bolstering the public purse and employing a multitude of individuals in the upholding of the law.

The scenario is representing 'The Forces of Nature & Nurture' and the process of trial and error relating to the great unknown manifested in our bodies and minds, which carries an associated 'Cost of Living'.

In the ultimate state of existence, the comfort zone may represent a narrow gap or thin line, whereby the 'Cost of Living' could not be reduced any further, and so we would have reached our goal in life.

This raises the question of our physical and mental predisposition and the potential problems associated with the limits manifested in our bodies as per the forces of Nature, and minds as per the forces of Nurture.

In the physical dimension, there are some 100,000 or so genes in every cell of our body, some of which are used all of the time, others may never be used, and some 4,200 represent diseases of the body.

A similar scenario applies to our metaphysical dimension as we can see in our personality traits, some of which are used all of the time, some may never be used, whilst some others represent diseases of the mind.

This brings us to the difference between the lower life forms and modern man insomuch that the life forms up to and including archaic man did not suffer from any mental diseases relating to their interaction needs.

The reason for this lies in our basic purpose in life and the predetermined body language, where the interaction needs were simply enforced with a 'Fight or Flight' mentality relating to the element of fairness.

Considering this was meant to ensure 'The Survival of the Fittest', the element of fairness was not only outside the genetically contrived fitness for purpose, but also beyond the cultural aims and objectives.

The self-determined language did not come into play until modern man appeared on the scene, upon which the human mind became interested in its ultimate purpose in life, for which it was duly equipped.

The phenomenon can be seen in the lowering of the larynx so as to facilitate a learned spoken language, the differentiation of the left and right brain functions and the emergence of the frontal lobes, and more.

And so our bodies and minds were now catering for a) Our Basic Purpose in Life and b) Our Ultimate Purpose in Life, the latter of which can be seen in the emergence of the businesses of industry and government.

As it stands, the businesses of industry and government are now catering for the adequacy of our basic needs and the fairness of our interaction needs, respectively, in which lies our difference to the animals.

At the same time, the business' pursuit of the great unknown is based on its perception of a 'Commercial Opportunity' relating to the creation of a product/service or a social control for which there is a demand.

In that context, it is important for us to differentiate between the diseases of the body and the mind, which may well be intertwined within the context of 'Our Ultimate Purpose in Life, but are different nevertheless.

That is, the stresses or problems relating to an unfair relationship or upbringing may well be manifested in the form of a physiological symptom that is designed to make us physically sick, or even kill us outright.

Yet the root cause(s) are entirely different to the basic needs of the body, in which case our misperception of reality is not going to solve the problem, which may even become manifested in the genes.

The phenomenon can be seen in the prolonged or excessive deprivation of our interaction needs during our formative years which may lead to a genetic mutation or 'rogue gene' relating to the lack of fairness.

At the same time, the 'rogue gene' is not found in every person, but when it does, it may lead to a psychopathic killer if and when the subconscious senses an opportunity to advertise the problem to the community.

Subject to the emotional impact of the symptom(s) on the community, the businesses of industry and/or government may attempt to solve the problem by removing the gene prior to, or during, the time of conception.

But then again, the gene was put there by Mother Nature so that we may learn from the symptoms relating to the deprivation of our interaction needs, and the same applies to the deprivation of our basic needs.

As a consequence, if we were to remove the genes relating to the diseases of the body or the mind without identifying and modifying the underlying causes, the rogue genes would simply reemerge in the future.

This raises the question of our responsibility for the various diseases, the purpose of which is to alert the businesses of industry and government with respect to elements of adequacy and fairness, respectively.

If we begin with the diseases of the body, our legal responsibility seems to be fairly lenient, as we can see in the diagnosis, treatment and prevention of diseases, illnesses, injury, and other physical impairments.

This takes us to the diseases of the mind, from the symptoms of depression to the psychopathic killer, the ultimate purpose of which is associated with "The Elements of Good & Evil", as illustrated below.

The Elements of Good & Evil

1) The 'Parasite' feeds on 'the naivety of its stakeholders;
2) The 'Predator' feeds on 'the vulnerability of its stakeholders'
3) The 'Paradox' sees only to 'the needs of <u>some</u> of its stakeholders';
4) The 'Panacea' sees to 'the need gratification of <u>all</u> of its stakeholders';
5. The 'Paradise' caters for 'the ongoing improvement of <u>all</u> its stakeholders'

Fig.: 1.1.2

The concept applies to a) the body where the cells and organs are the stakeholders and b) the mind where the individuals and the businesses of industry and government are the stakeholders.

As to the latter, the definition of a stakeholder refers to:

a) *a person, a group, an organization, a member or system which affects or can be affected by an organization's actions;*

b) *an entity that can be affected by the results of that in which they are said to be a stakeholder or 'have a stake'.*

As a consequence, any individual, competing group or competing organization may be deemed a stakeholder as they are, or can be, affected by another person's, group's or organization's actions, and vice versa.

The phenomenon is raising the question of our own bodies and the relationship between the billions of individual cells and the many organs of our body, none of which seem to be competing with each other.

The reason for this can only be related to the fact that the human body represents a model of consistency and completeness that is based on the knowledge of the distant past manifested in the genes.

At the same time, this knowledge is hardly adequate when it comes to our sustainability in the near and distant future as an individual and also as a human race that is becoming increasingly interdependent.

And so we are faced with 'The Elements of Good & Evil', which are ultimately designed to motivate us towards the 'Need to Change' our current disposition in life and possibly our 'Want to Compete' with others.

'The Elements of Good & Evil' can be seen in the evolution of life on earth, whereby the Parasites and Predators were the front runners in the evolutionary chain culminating in the creation of the genders.

In that context, the genders represent the emergence of new species and the mind, the purpose of which was to 'see only to the needs of some of its stakeholders', as in the members of that species.

And so the Paradox became the new model, where every new link in the chain of evolution was adapting to the environment of change and competition, as illustrated below under "The Process of Natural Selection".

The Process of Natural Selection

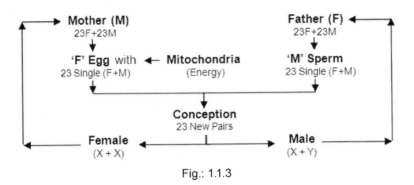

Fig.: 1.1.3

"The process of natural selection is based on the nucleus of each cell in our body containing two sets of 23 chromosomes representing the genetic information relating to our mother (23M) and our father. (23F)

Out of the 46 chromosomes, the egg and the sperm inherit only 23 chromosomes representing the mother and the father, which then make up two sets of 23 chromosomes at the time of conception.

A further Mitochondria is located outside the female egg, the purpose of which is to take in nutrients, break it down and create energy for the cell in line with the prevailing 'stable & predictable' patterns of life.

Whilst the chromosomes of the egg and the Mitochondria are fixed from the time of our mother's conception, the chromosomes of the male sperm are inherently variable subject to their continuous production".

The dynamic status of the male sperm is giving us an insight into the universal process of adaptation, whereby any real changes in the environment can be accommodated within a relatively short period of time.

If the sperm was only containing parental chromosomes without the introduction of a new gene, the adaptation would have been limited, as the information is confined to the knowledge of the distant past.

And whilst the process is claimed to apply to the adaptation of an existing species, it is also claimed to apply to the creation of an entirely new species, which has nothing to do with 'The Survival of the Fittest'.

Under the circumstances, even Darwin conceded that *'the evolution of life by numerous, successive and slight modifications'* had its limits, and so we are left to wonder about the creation of a new species and:

a) 'What universal forces decide on how many chromosomes are going to make up the nucleus of the female egg and the male sperm, and what are the characteristics relating to 'Our Ultimate Purpose in Life?"

b) "What universal forces decide on which of the 100,000 or so genes in every cell of our body are going to be activated with respect to our physical growth and development and basic purpose in life?"

c) "What universal forces decide on which personality trait associated with our mental capacity is going to be activated with respect to our intellectual growth and development and ultimate purpose in life?

In order to unravel the mystery, we have to step back and look at the big picture relating to 'Our Ultimate Purpose in Life', the reality of which began with the emergence of modern man some 200,000 years ago.

By 100,000 years ago, modern humans had moved along the Nile Valley and the coastlines of India and south eastern Asia and sailed to Australia.

About 40,000 years ago, modern man moved from north-eastern Africa into Europe and from south eastern Asia into eastern Asia, followed by their way to Siberia and Alaska and down to North and South America some 10,000 years ago.

Wherever modern man encountered their archaic counterparts in Africa, Asia and Europe, the old-style humans eventually disappeared.

The separation began when the modern hunter-gatherers organized themselves in groups called bands, consisting of a few closely related families, probably ten to fifty people altogether.

The groups had many good reasons for interacting with others such as trading tools, food, ideas and creating webs of mutual obligation, so that one band can rely on another during times of crises, forge alliances and protect territory and resources.

This would have certainly given modern man the upper hand, and eventually the monopoly as a human race, where the archaic model was of no further use, and so it disappeared from the face of the earth.

Because of the benefits to be gained by interacting, bands throughout history have tended to organize themselves into larger units traditionally labelled as tribes, which is covering a broad range of social structures.

The bands within a tribe may live close to each other, or they may gather at a central location periodically to exchange goods and to intermarry, where the language was usually the same.

More broadly, they typically share a way of life and a belief system uniting them for more than 100,000 years until the invention of agriculture some 12,000 years ago near the eastern Mediterranean shoreline.

Instead of continually moving from place to place, they began to live in single places for much or all of the year, where they learned to exploit the wild plants and animals in an area much more intensively.

Once people became sedentary, they didn't have to haul their possessions from one camp to another, which also allowed them to acquire more tools such as heavy stone mortars used to grind grain.

They made cups and bowls and stored goods in pits lined with stone slabs and experimented with seeds of chickpeas, lentils, wheat and barley and the domestication of livestock.

Sometime between 10,000 and 9,000 years ago, the people of Jericho built a 10 foot wide and 13 foot high wall around their town, with a moat outside that was 30 feet wide and 10 feet deep.

Whilst the purpose of the wall was to defend the city against marauding armies, it signalled a dedication to communal life and the willingness to work together towards a common good.

The Jericho experiment heralds a social organization and population that was stable and growing slowly, given the children didn't have to be able to walk before a woman can have another that she can carry.

The resulting population growth was dramatic, growing from 6 million right before the invention of agriculture to some 250 million by the first century A.D. reflecting a new species of human beings.

The invention of agriculture changed our life as the domestication of plants and animals led to the expansion of populations, cities, warfare, nations, mass religion and a growing reliance on the forces of Nurture.

So how does this help us with respect to the questions of "What universal forces decide the how and why we live on this planet?"

The answer lies in the similarity between the lower life forms up to and including archaic man and the maturation of the female egg in our mother's womb, both of which are essentially driven by 'The Survival of the Fittest'.

<u>Note:</u> The phrase 'survival of the fittest' was first used by Mr. Herbert Spencer in his 1864 book The Principles of Biology and thereafter promoted by Charles Darwin in his 1869 book Origin of Species. Today, many credit Darwin with this phrase.

As to the mature female egg, the focus changes suddenly with the fertilization of the egg, upon which it begins to multiply as if out of control before differentiating in the context of the emerging organs of the foetus.

At the same time, the interaction needs of the cells and organs are suddenly coming into play as the forces of Nature are constructing the life form according to a predetermined process of universal creation.

A similar scenario applies to 'The Human Condition' and the emergence of modern man, upon which the human race multiplied as if out of control before constructing the businesses of industry and government.

Under the circumstances, the interaction needs were suddenly becoming an integral part of the creative process, whereby the nature of the interaction depended on the growing mental capacity of the human race.

So where does this leave us other than to assume that the essence of our existence here on earth, or 'Ultimate Purpose in Life', is to create a cosmic foetus according to a predetermined process of universal creation?

The concept is not entirely new as we can see in the story of Adam and Eve who were expelled from 'The Garden of Eden' because they ate from 'The Tree of the Knowledge of the Good and the Evil'.

In doing so, they were suddenly able to decide what is good and what is evil as they applied themselves to the pursuit of the great unknown so as to advance the human race, using the process of trial & error.

In that context, Adam and Eve would have already been able to decide what is good and what is bad when it came to the adequacy of their basic needs, which was now extended to the element of fairness.

By the same token, if it hadn't been for the metaphysical element of fairness, the human race would have never been able to multiply and specialize in the context of the businesses of industry and government.

Note: The proposition of the 'cosmic foetus' is based on the assumption that Eve represents the mature cosmic egg, whilst Adam is meant to represent the cosmic sperm, both of which were effectively in Paradise.

That is, their existence in the cosmic reproductive system is as close to a Paradise as we can imagine, especially when we consider the fact that our problems only began with the emergence of modern man.

This brings us back to 'The Elements of Good & Evil' and the diseases of the mind, the primary purpose of which is to advertise the deprivation of our interaction needs as an expression of our mental capacity.

And so we are right back to where we started with the definition of 'Our Ultimate Purpose in Life', whereby *"the degree of our problems at any one time is proportionate to the perception of reality by one and all"*.

On that note, let us have a closer look at our mental capacity and the claim that:

Humans are multi-dimensional beings composed of many parts and with connections to many dimensions, where the human as well as the universe is far more complex than scientists would have us believe.

In that context, physics is the science of the physical realm and its laws and functions, whilst metaphysics is the science of all realms and their laws and functions.

The claim is further supported by the definition of life, according to which:

"Living objects have signalling and self-sustaining processes which non-living objects do not, either because the functions have ceased (death), or because they lack the functions.

A complex living system is called an organism which undergoes metabolism, maintains homeostasis, possesses a capacity to grow, responds to stimuli, reproduces and adapts to its environment over generations."

This is further extended by the definition of an ecosystem, whereby:

An ecosystem is a community of living organisms (plants, animals and microbes) in conjunction with the nonliving components of their environment (things like air, water and mineral soil), interacting as a system.

These living organisms and nonliving components are regarded as linked together through nutrient cycles and energy flows.

As ecosystems are defined by the network of interactions among organisms and between organisms and their environment, they can come in any size but usually encompass specific, limited spaces. (Some scientists even say that the entire planet is an ecosystem)

We might even suggest that the galaxies (if not the entire universe) resemble ecosystems that undergo metabolism, maintain homeostasis, possess a capacity to grow, respond to stimuli, reproduce and adapt.

After all, why should 'The Forces of Nature & Nurture', 'The Elements of Good & Evil', 'The Process of Natural Selection', the creation of new species and the sciences of physics and metaphysics apply only to us?

If this was to be the case, "What is the Point of Living?" when we are only going to die with the planet earth, as we are bound to do unless we come to grips with 'Our Ultimate Purpose in Life' and get on with it.

In order to clarify our role within the cosmic scheme of things, let us consider the following options, whereby:

1. The mind is the same as the brain and predetermined from conception onwards.
2. The mind is different to the brain and continues to grow from conception onwards.
3. The mind is different to the brain and continues to grow during one life after another.

1. The first option is based on the assumption that the mind is a consumable which is not unlike a computer that is discarded upon our natural death, upon which it is returned to its rudimentary components.

Under the circumstances, the mind or brain would have been programmed with respect to the basic needs and the interaction needs, in which case 'it' would not have any kind of responsibility or feelings.

2. The second option is much more acceptable from a learning point of view, in which case we would have a responsibility and feelings relating to the satisfaction of our basic needs and our interaction needs.

Without this metaphysical aspect of our being, we would have never been able to develop new skills and habits and evolve, nor would we have been able to benefit from the trials and errors of our forefathers.

3. This brings us to the third and final option and only possible explanation of our role within the cosmic scheme of things, whereby the mind of modern man is nevertheless different to that of the lower life forms.

That is, if our role was represented by option two, we would have never seen fit to criticise, or improve on, the accrued knowledge of our forefathers or created the businesses of industry and government.

To all intents and purposes, we would have never evolved beyond the level of archaic man, who might have survived and thrived at the top of the food chain, but was nevertheless destined to die with the planet earth.

At the same time, archaic man was not interested in the pursuit of any knowledge beyond 'The Survival of the Fittest', in which case it was representing option two until modern man appeared on the human scene.

As to the other life forms, the food chain was primarily aimed at sustaining the physical dimension of the cosmic egg, whilst "The Evolution of the Vertebrates" was designed to evolve the human race, as illustrated below.

The Evolution of the Vertebrates

| Fish | Amphibian | Bird | Rabbit | Human |

Fig.: 1.1.4

It so happens, none of the 'links' in the food chain are based on their need to adapt to the environment, if not the reverse, as the survival of the amphibian would have been less secure than that of the fish.

Likewise, the evolution of the bird is not a consequence of a lizard wanting to fly, but rather the forces of Nature and their intimate knowledge of the 'Grand Order of Design' relating to the evolution of life on earth.

This takes us back to Darwin conceding that *'the evolution of life by numerous, successive and slight modifications'* had its limits, which is further demonstrated by the natural gap between the evolving species.

That is, if the new species was based on *'numerous, successive and slight modifications',* then there would have been a traceability of these steps as in the living reminders of the process or fossil evidence.

After all, every successive and slight modification would have been able to survive in its own right if it was to lead to the next step, and so on, yet there is no evidence of this misperception of reality.

And so we come to the conclusion that the forces of Nature had to be involved with respect to the creation of a new species, the need for, and Nature of which, can only be associated with a 'Grand Order of Design'.

In doing so, the first vertebrate did not accidentally lend itself to the creation of increasingly complex life forms that happened to look much the same at the early stage and then grew into something entirely different.

Instead, it represents a vision of the distant future that was bound to culminate in the evolution or creation of archaic man, the physical and mental capacity of which represented the maturation of the cosmic egg.

By the same token, the evolution of archaic man and the need for a large brain is not so much aimed at our survival here on earth, but rather the remote possibility of our having to survive somewhere in the universe.

1.2   The Nature of the Universe

On that note, let us look at the physical makeup of the universe or ordinary matter, which is subjected to the gravitational pull versus the metaphysical representing the dark energy and dark matter, which are not.

That is, according to the Planck mission team and the standard model of cosmology, the total mass—energy of the universe contains 4.9% ordinary matter, 26.8% dark matter and 68.3% dark energy.

The dark energy is furthermore divided into the constant energy (passive forces) and the dynamic energy (active forces) which permeates all of space and tends to accelerate the expansion of the universe.

If we convert the above into a meaningful relationship between the metaphysical intelligence and the building blocks of life, we are beginning to get a glimpse of "The Nature of the Universe", as illustrated below.

The Nature of the Universe

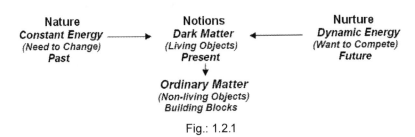

Fig.: 1.2.1

The illustration portrays the universe with respect to the elements of time and space and the associated plight of the *"Living objects and the signalling and self-sustaining processes which non-living objects do not."*

Hence, depending on where and when the object lives here on earth or in the universe, the signalling and self-sustaining processes of the organism reflect the knowledge of the past, the present and the future.

The living and non-living objects are part of a 'Grand Order of Design' whereby the forces of Nature represent the knowledge of the past and the 'Need to Change', and Nurture the future and the 'Want to Compete'.

At the same time, the two forces are not in a position to act on their own volition, as they are inherently biased when it comes to 'their' role within the cosmic scheme of things, which takes us to the forces of Notion.

We can appreciate the elements of time and space when we consider the remarkable history of the crocodile which hasn't changed much (if at all) in millions of years, which is in stark contrast to the human race.

Yet, despite the fact that the crocodile and other living objects didn't 'Need to Change' over millions of years, they are still subjected to the 'Want to Compete' with other members of their species and life forms.

This brings us to the forces of Notions and the elements of change and competition, for which we need a physical brain or computer and a metaphysical mind to convert the mental images into a meaningful conduct.

To begin with, let us have a look at the forces of Nature and our 'Need to Change' our bodies and minds from the time of our conception to the time of our natural death, representing:

1. The 'stable & predictable' patterns of life that can be administered unconsciously by the information manifested in our inherited genes.
2. The 'unstable but predictable' patterns that can be administered subconsciously by the information manifested in our skills and habits.
3. The 'unstable & unpredictable' patterns that can only be addressed with a conscious awareness of the potential gains and/or losses.

Under the circumstances, the mind has Notions and Emotions relating to the 'unstable & unpredictable' patterns of life which will cause it to pursue the great unknown in line with its perception of reality.

And as the behaviour is proving itself useful and the pattern is identified as an 'unstable but predictable' pattern, it may lead to the development of a subconscious skill or habit that can always be changed.

A similar scenario applies to the manifestation of the skill or habit in the genes if and when they emerge as a 'stable & predictable' means of survival, whereby the decision to do so is up to the forces of Nature.

Under the circumstances, the forces of Nature would have to be well versed with the 'ins' and 'outs' of a 'Grand Order of Design' relating to the evolution of life here on earth and also in the greater universe.

This brings us to the forces of Nurture and our 'Want to Compete' for:

1. The limited resources here on earth and in the universe so as to maintain the nutrient cycle from the time of conception to the time of death.
2. The privilege to change the genes by way of sexual intercourse so as to adapt the life forms to the accrued changes in the environment.
3. The creation of new and exciting products/services and social controls so as to facilitate the growth and development of the cosmic foetus.

For all we know, the elements of change and competition represent the essence of life, the reality of which goes well beyond our planet and our universe, which is really mindboggling when we think about it.

Note: If there had been an unlimited supply of nutrients here on earth and in the universe, the 'Want to Compete' would have never arisen in the first place, nor would there have been a universal need to die.

After all, the only reason why we have to die is associated with our need to keep up with, or ahead of, the nearest competitor, without which the forces of Nature could have easily rendered us an eternal state of being.

That is, the 'Need to Change' in response to the three levels of variability does not require a new body, but rather a change in its make up, in which case the cyclic renewal of the cells should be sufficient.

It is true that individual cells have a finite life span, and when they die off they are replaced with new cells, as The New York Public Library's Science Desk Reference notes, "There are between 50 and 75 trillion cells in the body.

Each type of cell has its own life span, and when a human dies it may take hours or days before all the cells in the body die." (Forensic investigators take advantage of this vaguely morbid fact when determining the cause and time of death of homicide victims.)

Red blood cells live for about four months, white blood cells live on average more than a year, skin cells live about two or three weeks whilst colon cells have it rough: They die off after about four days.

Sperm cells have a life span of only about three days, while brain cells typically last an entire lifetime (neurons in the cerebral cortex, for example, are not replaced when they die).

On the other hand, the "Benjamin Button" jellyfish which is only about as wide as the nail on our little finger has the uncanny ability to reverse and then restart its life cycle.

After it spawns, the adult can reabsorb its tentacles into its body and then form a shell to resemble its first stage as a polyp. The polyp then makes more jellyfish.

The lobster is another one of a select few species that do not seem to decline with age, like most other creatures, though still susceptible to predators and fishermen. It's unclear just how long lobsters can live, and some scientists think that, if a lobster is lucky enough to avoid predators, it could potentially live forever.

At the same time, the lobster and the jellyfish would not be able to adapt to the environment, as they are not subjected to 'The Process of Natural Selection', which puts a bit of a dampener on our desire to live forever.

As to the dream of an eternal physical life for the human race, this will come to a gradual halt as the planet earth reaches the end of its cycle of life and death, like the entire universe will eventually come to an end.

On that note, let us have a look at 'The Big Bang Theory', whereby discoveries in astronomy and physics have shown that our universe did not only have a beginning, but it is also going through a cycle of life and death.

The accepted standard theory is an effort to explain what happened during and after that moment, according to which our universe sprang into existence as a "singularity" around 13.7 billion years ago.

At the same time, nobody seems to know for certain what a "singularity" is other than the general agreement that they represent zones within the universe which defy our current understanding of physics.

Yet they are thought to exist at the core of "black holes" or areas of gravitational pressure thought to be so intense that finite matter is squeezed into infinite density. (a concept that truly boggles the mind).

Nobody knows where the "singularity" came from or why it appeared other than it began with a Big Bang and apparently inflated, expanded and cooled, as illustrated below under "The Universal Cycle of Life & Death".

The Universal Cycle of Life & Death

1   The Big Bang
2   The radiation-dominated period
3   The matter-dominated period
4   The dark energy–dominated period
5   The contraction period
6   The big crunch

Fig.: 1.2.2

Note: The Universal Cycle of Life & Death is based on the ekpyrotic model of the universe which is an alternative to the standard cosmic inflation model for the very early universe.

Whilst both models accommodate the standard Big Bang Lambda-CDM model of our universe, the ekpyrotic model is a precursor to, and part of, some cyclic models.

The ekpyrotic model came out of work by Neil Turok and Paul Steinhardt and maintains that the universe did not start in a singularity, but came about from the collision of two branes. (a mathematical concept that appears in string theory and related theories.

There are many misconceptions surrounding 'The Big Bang Theory', whereby some experts say there was no explosion, but rather a continual expansion like a balloon expands from an infinitesimally small beginning.

The debate continued as three British astrophysicists (Steven Hawking, George Ellis and Roger Penrose) turned their attention to the 'Theory of Relativity' and its implications on the notion of a Big Bang at the time.

In 1968 and 1970, the trio published a number of papers in which they extended Einstein's Theory of General Relativity to include calculations that time and space began with the origin of matter and energy.

On that note, let us to go back some 4.6 billion years ago here on earth when there was widespread Volcanism with photosynthetic algae bringing about the steady build-up of atmospheric oxygen.

And whilst the atmospheric oxygen does not represent life, the earliest unmistakeable record of life dates back some 3.4 billion years ago in the form of layers of calcium carbonate built up by blue-green algae.

This was followed by the evolution of the first single celled organisms with nuclei some 1.5 billion years ago, where the 'stable & predictable' patterns of life were manifested in the (unconscious) genes.

The concept of the genes allowed Mother Nature to evolve the food chain beginning with the predatory single cells some 800 million years ago, and the first multi-cellular animals some 590 million years ago.

<u>*Note*</u>: *Every organism in the food chain needs to obtain energy in order to live, whereby all plants get their energy from the sun whilst some animals eat the plants and some animals eat other animals.*

A food chain is the sequence of who eats whom in a biological community (an ecosystem) to obtain nutrition, starting with the primary energy source, usually the sun or boiling-hot deep sea vents.

This brings us to the second level insomuch that Mother Nature created a '<u>subconscious</u>' for the purpose of recording the experiences of the life form in order to identify the '<u>unstable but predictable</u>' patterns of life.

The recording would have started at the time of conception, upon which the 'subconscious' would have been able to develop skills and habits so as to protect the life form against the environment of change.

Under the circumstances, the survival and protection of the life forms was essentially based on the distant past and recent past, respectively, which posed a problem insomuch that both were based on hindsight.

And so Mother Nature created the third level of life in the form of the '<u>conscious</u>', whose basic role in life was to deal with the present moment in time and the prevailing '<u>unstable & unpredictable</u>' patterns of life.

In order to do so, the life forms were given a gender, basic needs, basic senses, interaction needs, a self-determining mind and the power to deploy the body with respect to the basic needs and interaction needs.

The phenomenon represents a quantum leap in the evolutionary process, as none of the features would have made any sense on their own, like the creation of a female gender without a male counterpart.

Likewise, the basic needs and the basic senses would not have made any sense without the interaction needs and a self-determining mind and power to override the subconscious and the unconscious, if necessary.

Finally, the self-determination would not have made any sense unless the behaviour was influenced by a set of feelings relating to the comfort zone and the limits imposed by 'The Forces of Nature & Nurture'.

This brings us back to the food chain which is starting with a species that eats no other species and ends with a species that is eaten by no other species", as illustrated below under "The Survival of the Fittest".

The Survival of the Fittest

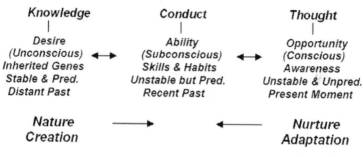

Fig.: 1.2.3

The illustration portrays the principles underlying thought, conduct, knowledge and the nature of the universe with respect to the forces of Nature and creation of life versus Nurture and the adaptation of life.

In doing so, the forces of Nurture did not come into play until the arrival of the conscious mind and its powers of self-determination relating to the prevailing opportunities for 'The Survival of the Fittest'.

The evolution of the unconscious, the subconscious and the conscious is furthermore supported by the evolution of the human brain, whereby:

1. The brain stem links up to the spinal cord regulating functions such as heart rate and blood flow, eye movement, pupil size and the mid brain controlling eye, neck and head movement.

The function of the brain stem is entirely associated with the 'stable & predictable' patterns of life relating to the distant past manifested in the genes.

2. The cerebellum is located at the back of the brain and controls balance and muscular co-ordination, thus allowing precise control during activities such as walking and running.

The function of the cerebellum is associated with the 'unstable but predictable' patterns of life relating to the recent past manifested in our skills & habits.

3. The cerebrum forms the left and right hemispheres of the brain, which are responsible for functions including speech, memory, consciousness and logical and emotional thought.

The function of the cerebrum is associated with the 'unstable & unpredictable' patterns of life relating to the present manifested in our conscious awareness.

This brings us to the fertilization of the mature cosmic egg, or emergence of modern man and the lowering of the larynx (to facilitate a spoken language) and the development of the frontal lobes of the brain.

"The frontal lobes are the seat of emotions and judgments related to sympathy or the ability to feel sorrow for someone else's suffering and empathy, which is the ability to understand another's feelings and problems.

They are also the seat of understanding humour, including subtle witticisms and word plays, as well as recognizing sarcasm and irony; and they are also where the recognition of deception occurs.

The frontal lobes control the processes called "mentalizing" upon which our socialization is based; this is the ability to understand another's mental processes.

Other functions that the frontal lobes control are the functioning of sequencing events, which is the ability to plan a series of movements needed to perform a multi-step task, like making a sandwich.

The spontaneity of facial expression and of interaction with others is also controlled by the frontal lobes as is the function of flexibility in thinking processes, for example, being able to conceive of and choose between complex alternatives in a social environment.

The problematic opposite of this flexibility is perseverance or fixed persistence of a single thought, focus on a single task and resistance to emotional liability, which is commonly referred to as mood changes or mood swings.

The ability to solve problems, which often depends on flexible thinking and the ability to correctly express language are both controlled by the frontal lobes, as well.

In addition to this, our personalities are controlled by the frontal lobes as they also control movement, initiation, emotional impulsivity, memory, sexual behaviour, and judgment.

At the same time, the lobes are not identical in function, as the left lobe is most predominantly language related and the source of logic while the right lobe is most predominantly non-verbal and creative.

In fact we may know or be an artist who cannot respond verbally while immersed in the creative—right brain, non-verbal—process, however, it is significant to note that modern technological advances in MRIs, PETs and CT Scans show that many people pose exceptions to this left/right divide because their brains involve both lobes in nearly all behaviours.

The frontal lobes are of paramount significance in determining our daily capabilities, personality manifestations, social interactions and judgments and decisions, which makes the frontal lobes indeed the seat of our essence and nature."

These characteristics are certainly not associated with the behaviour of archaic man, which tends to reinforce the proposition of a connection between a 'Grand Order of Design' and 'The Human Condition'.

But what does this really mean like, are we the catalyst to the creation of another galaxy, where the pursuit of the great unknown is simply associated with 'its' need to adapt to the universal environment of changes and competition?

If so, our Solar System would have to represent the womb of a female galaxy, in which case the human race may represent the first in a line of universal creations that began many billions of years ago.

That is, there is strong evidence that the solar system formed about 4.6 billion years ago and it took about 500 million years for the planets to form in more or less their current location and orbits around the sun.

By the same token, the sun has another 5.5 billion years before it dies out, in which case it may still have another universal creation left in the context of the solar system and fertilization of another cosmic egg.

Let us explore the options relating to the proposition of a living universal environment, where the elements of change and competition are just as ruthless and rampant as they are here on earth, whereby:

1. Our universe is the only one that has ever been and ever will be— end of story.
2. Everything about life and death and beyond should be left to the belief systems.
3. Our universe is an incomprehensible phenomenon that has no rhyme or reason.

1. If the first option was to be true, we would have to wonder about the incredible intelligence relating to the creation of the universe and the complexity of the life forms and the elements of change and competition.

This was obviously not an accident, nor was it developed on the run, which seems to indicate that there is a 'Grand Order of Design' that may be well beyond our current knowledge, but that could soon change.

After all, 'We' are the meat in the sandwich when it comes to our role within the cosmic scheme of things as we represent the 'Dark Matter' and powers of 'Notion' with respect to 'The Nature of the Universe'.

2. If the second option was to be true, we would have to wonder about our notions and emotions relating to our interaction needs and our desire and ability to create the businesses of industry and government.

In doing so, we were no longer tied to the single-minded pursuit of our basic needs, as 'The Survival of the Fittest' was now competing with 'The Survival of the Fairest' representing a battle of Nature and Nurture.

In the process, many belief systems are having a final go at the sustainability of their misperceptions of reality as they proclaim themselves beyond scientific analysis and become a Parasite to the community.

3. And whilst the belief systems represent the extreme in one direction, the total rejection of a supernatural involvement with our being on this planet and 'The Nature of the Universe' is equally offensive and ignorant.

That is not to say, the rejection of the belief in the existence of a deity or deities is offensive or ignorant, but rather the extremity of that rejection to the point where they are affecting 'Our Ultimate Purpose in Life'.

Furthermore, the mere suggestion that there is no rhyme or reason when it comes to the complexity of life and the proposition of a higher purpose than 'The Survival of the Fittest' is an insult to our intelligence.

And so we rest our case as we continue with our pursuit of the great unknown relating 'The Nature of the Universe' as a reflection of our role within the cosmic scheme of things, or dark matter looking for the light.

On that note, let us consider the common observational wisdom among astronomers that there are 17 billion Earth-sized planets in our galaxy and, whilst they do not yet know how many of these are inhabitable zones, the implications of this discovery are astounding.

Simply put: If there are 17 billion Earth-sized worlds in our galaxy alone, it's clear that the Universe has the potential to be teeming with life, (according to the astronomers) but this may not hold up in reality.

That is, if our Solar system is the womb of a female galaxy, the so called 'life' would be restricted to the planet earth, whereas the remaining planets and stars are simply a part of a higher form of universal being

In that context, the planets and stars have a life span that is not unlike our cells, where the 'Want to Compete' does not actually come into play as all the cells and organs are part of a complete universal ecosystem.

By the same token, there may be other female galaxies out there with maturing or fertilized eggs at varying degrees of gestation, in which case the 'life' forms are deemed to be similar to those on our planet earth.

The entire debate about life on earth and somewhere out there is based on the acceptance of our metaphysical dimension and the 'Need to Change' versus the 'Want to Compete' pervading throughout the universe.

This takes us to the alleged UFO (Unidentified Flying Objects) sightings, of which there have been thousands over the past millennium or so, including supposed cases of reported close encounters and abductions.

And whilst some of the sightings turned out to be natural phenomena, misperceptions of reality and hoaxes to entertain or confuse the public, the phenomenon of the UFO is difficult to ignore altogether.

Sceptics in the scientific community resist the evidence for extraterrestrial visitation because of the implications it raises, yet the answer lies in the incentive structure of the analyst and his or desire to believe, or not.

Hence, an intelligent non-scientist who has neither incentive nor predisposition to favour one type of reality over the other may pursue the great unknown, whilst a scientist may reject the claim outright or ignore it.

For scientists, it would open a whole new problem domain, and it would make them look incompetent in the public's eyes for missing out on this fact for 50 years, and so the incentive is to wait until they get irrefutable physical proof.

Their incentive structure prohibits them from making any such inference unless it is unavoidable, and they will strain the boundaries of logic and reason to no end to dismiss all evidence other than physical proof, no matter how powerful it may be.

This scientific predisposition toward disbelief, rooted not in science and logic but rather in dogma and paradigm, brings us to the logical trickery of the scientific UFO debunker.

In view of the above, let us propose another theory relating to the creation of a cosmic foetus, whereby the solar system represents the womb of a female galaxy that is displaying a natural desire for sex.

As a consequence, the chances of a male galaxy injecting its semen into our solar system in the form of an unidentified flying object may not be all that difficult to imagine, including the encounters and abductions.

The possibility would shed some light on the appearance of Adam some 200,000 years ago, after which the human physiology changed suddenly with the lowering of the larynx and the development of the frontal lobes.

In that context, the story of Adam and Eve may well represent a 'Close Encounters of the Third Kind', as portrayed in the true story and film by Steven Spielberg which re-awakened our fascination with the eternal question—are we alone in the universe?

The movie follows three central characters—Roy Neary who develops an obsession after sighting a UFO, Jillian Guiler, a single mother whose son is abducted by aliens and Claude Lacombe, a scientist working on a secret government project to establish First Contact with the extra-terrestrials.

Although it is a work of fiction, this sci-fi fantasy—including the legendary UFO road chase scene—was in fact inspired by real people, real science and real-life witness testimonies.

To ensure the film was as accurate as possible to the reported cases, Spielberg hired Dr J Allen Hynek who was widely considered to be the authority on the scientific analysis of the UFO phenomenon.

Hynek, who came up with the UFO classification system which *Close Encounters of the Third Kind* takes its title from, was originally an astronomer and was hired by the US Air Force to look into the growing number of UFO reports that arose in the late forties.

As sightings became more prevalent, the US government came under pressure to set up a formal body to study the cases—its main goal was to determine if any of these sightings were a threat to the American people.

Dr Hynek served as the organization's scientific advisor and his role was to look into the truly inexplicable cases and try to explain them, but the more cases he looked at, the more his position changed from a firm sceptic to a believer in the unexplained.

In the Project Bluebook's seventeen year history, he oversaw the investigation of over 12,000 reported sightings from all over the United States in its seventeen-year history.

This takes to the other scientific obsession with, or rejection of, life on other planets in our universe or 'Extraterrestrial Life' which is defined as life that does not originate from Earth.

It is also referred to as alien life, or simply aliens referring to forms of life ranging from simple bacteria-like organisms to beings far more complex than humans.

The development and testing of hypotheses on extraterrestrial life is known as exobiology or astrobiology; the term astrobiology, however, includes the study of life on Earth viewed in its astronomical context.

The scientists at the National Institutes of Health reported studies that life in the universe may have begun "9.7±2.5 billion years ago", billions of years before the Earth was formed, based on extrapolating the "genetic complexity of organisms" to earlier times.

Many scientists consider extraterrestrial life to be plausible, but there is no direct evidence of its existence despite the ongoing search for signs of extraterrestrial life, from radios used to detect possible extraterrestrial signals, to telescopes used to search for potentially habitable extra solar planets.

Apart from the 'stable & predictable' patterns of life manifested in our genes and the unlikely compatibility of our survival needs with the new conditions, there is also the question of our metaphysical dimension.

That is, our need to migrate to another planet would have been associated with our failure to complete our mission on this planet, not because of a nutritional shortfall, but of our inability to get along with our fellow man.

Under the circumstances, that flaw in our human nature would still be with us, regardless of our social status and accumulated wealth and ability to book a seat in the extraterrestrial vehicle or shuttle bus.

And if we think of creating an extraterrestrial bubble of life somewhere in the universe, whereby we are recreating the conditions of life here on earth in a sustainable fashion, let us think again.

And the same applies to the misperception of reality relating to our 'Death in the Deep Freeze', or cryonics, whereby the body may retain its integrity for a period of time, but the mind is not going to do the same.

And even if our mind happened to be available at the time of our reintroduction to life, how is the subconscious and unconscious information relating to our last life going to help us fit in with the new environment?

To all intents and purposes, we would probably wish we had never engaged in such a human process of trial and error, that is, unless we like to be put in a cage and observed by the scientists at the time.

1.3   The Metaphysical Aspects

At this point in time, let us continue with our attempt to unravel the mystery of life by way of focusing on our metaphysical dimension and transition from a 'Matter over Mind' status to a 'Mind over Matter' status.

The word 'metaphysics' is notoriously hard to define, whereby twentieth-century phrases like 'meta-language' and 'metaphilosophy' give the impression that metaphysics is a study that somehow "goes beyond" physics.

And whilst the phrases represent a study that is devoted to matters that transcend the mundane concerns of Newton, Einstein and Heisenberg, this impression is largely mistaken by the modern sciences.

The word 'metaphysics' is derived from a collective title of the fourteen books by Aristotle that we currently consider making up "Aristotle's Metaphysics", where even Aristotle himself did not know the word.

At the same time, Aristotle had four names for the branch of philosophy that is the subject-matter of his interpretation of Metaphysics, representing 'first philosophy', 'first science', 'wisdom', and 'theology'.

At least one hundred years after Aristotle's death, an editor of his works entitled those fourteen books "the after the physicals" or "the ones after the physical ones", being the books containing 'Aristotle's Physics'.

Another source refers to Metaphysics as two types of inquiry whereby the first aims to be the most general investigation possible and the question "are there principles applying to everything that is real?"

The second type of inquiry seeks to uncover "What is ultimately real?" which is frequently offering answers that are in sharp contrast to our everyday life and experiences from our conception to our death.

In that context, science is regarded as a catalogue of selected perceptions of realities that are acknowledged to be scientific and structured by means of concepts and theories or conscious experiences.

History is also regarded as a construct from conscious experiences and perceptions of reality relating to the concepts without the influence of an ego or bias relating to the present moment.

On that note, let us define the science of Metaphysics in the light of our discussions thus far and 'Our Ultimate Purpose in Life' in particular, as illustrated below under "The Metaphysical Aspects".

The Metaphysical Aspects

Level	Dimensions	Modes of Behaviour	Function	Reference
1	Unconscious	Acquire Fitness for Purpose	Automation	CEU
2	Subconscious	Protect Acquired Fitness	Adaptation	SOUL
3	Conscious	Find Application for Fitness	Anticipation	MIND
4	Super-conscious	Apply Fitness to Purpose	Aspirations	SELF
5	Social Conscience	Consider Greater Fitness	Administration	DEU

Fig.: 1.3.1

The illustration is portraying the Modes of Behaviour in the context of 'The Nature of The Universe' and the 'Need to Change' (1-3) and the 'Want to Compete' (3-5) until the universe is running out of building blocks.

Beginning with the phenomenon of our unconscious intelligence and acquisition of a fitness for purpose:

1. The forces of Nature represent the 'Constant Energy of the Universe' or 'CEU' for short, the reality of which can be seen in the evolution of the food chain, where each link has a fitness for a specific purpose.

In that context, the basic needs of the life forms are automatically catered for by the information manifested in the inherited genes representing the 'stable & predictable' patterns of life of the distant past.

In order to so, the forces of Nature are not only representing the knowledge dating back to the beginning of our planet earth, but furthermore the beginning of our universe and all the other universes before it.

Under the circumstances, Mother Nature would not only have full knowledge of everything that transpired, but also a thorough understanding of the 'Grand Order of Design' and ongoing universal life.

At the same time, Mother Nature is unable to deal directly with every life form in the universe from the time of their conception to the time of their natural death, as we can see in her delegation of that responsibility.

2. This brings us to the subconscious and the protection of our fitness by a 'Seeker of Ongoing Universal Life', (through Change) or 'SOUL', the purpose of which is to focus on the experiences of the recent past.

In that context, the protection of the life form is catered for semi-automatically whilst the 'SOUL' caters for its adaptation to the emerging 'unstable but predictable' environment of change and competition, or culture.

And if the skills and/or habits happen to turn into a 'stable & predictable' means of sustaining the life forms, they may be incorporated into the male genes and thereafter subjected to 'The Process of Natural Selection'.

But then again, they may not, as we can see in the creation of the spoken language, which may be 'stable & predictable' relating to a given people or location here on earth, but certainly not the human race as a whole.

Under the circumstances, we can only assume that Mother Nature knows what she is doing when it comes to which gene is going to be continued, and which skill or habit is going to be manifested in the male sperm.

3. This takes us to the purpose of 'our' existence here on earth as a 'Metaphysical Intelligence for the Notional Deployment' of the body, or 'MIND' for short, which is certainly not the same as the human brain.

In that context, the conscious 'Mind' is in touch with the subconscious which, in turn, is in touch with the unconscious, as we can see in the connection between the brainstem, the cerebellum and the cerebrum.

In the process, the conscious can override the subconscious skills and habits which, in turn, can override the inherited genes, all of which is adding up to a systematic delegation of authorities and responsibilities.

By the same token, if and when the conscious gets it wrong with respect to its powers of anticipation relating to the present moment, it will be informed with a suitable pressure from within and/or without.

The phenomenon can be seen in our notions and emotion before, during and after our deployment of the body, in line with our imagined expectations of a potential gain or a loss, as the case may be.

4. This takes us to the role of the super-conscious or 'Seeker of Eternal Life and Fulfillment', (through Competition) or 'SELF', the primary purpose of which is to create products/services for which there is a demand.

In doing so, the symptoms relating to the forces of Nature are high on the list of priorities as the creative efforts are initially designed to redress the problems relating to the basic needs of the community at large.

In the process, the individual may experience a degree of 'Eternal Life and Fulfillment' as the creative aspect of its personality will be remembered for as long as there is a need for the products and/or services.

The material and immaterial rewards associated with that kind of 'applied fitness' is bound to create an environment of competition which, in turn, may have a positive or negative impact on the element of change.

That is, the aspirations of the 'SELF' may not always be honourable, nor may they be always designed to benefit the community at large, as we can witness in the history of the human race and the elements of Evil.

5. This brings us to the role of the social conscience and 'Dynamic Energy of the Universe' or 'DEU' for short, the phenomenon of which represents the ongoing growth and development of the human mind.

As a consequence, the aspirations of the 'SELF' may have been extended to include the element of fairness relating to the interaction needs of the community, if need be, at the expense of the physical body.

This may include the individual or 'SELF' having benefitted from the unfair exploitation of others to the point where he or she may have developed a social conscience and desire to give back to the community.

By the same token, the same individual may see an even greater opportunity to exploit the community by way of manipulating the system and developing a power 'over' the bodies and/or minds of the people.

After all, such is the process of trial and error, according to which we may never know the difference between good and evil unless somebody starts the ball rolling with a potential problem like a Parasite or Predator.

In saying so, we are not suggesting the concept of a Parasite or a Predator is to be promoted, if not revered as a model of social contribution and behaviour, but rather the fact that it is a necessary component of life.

In order to clarify the matter, let us assume that the people of the world are living side by side and sharing their resources in a fair and adequate manner without argument, whilst accepting each others views.

In doing so, they would not have been motivated to pursue the great unknown so as to advance the human race, considering there were few problems which would have been easily solved by the community.

You might even say that the world was living in a virtual Paradise, that is, until the potential problems caught up with the misperception of reality in the form of actual problems that were about to wipe out the human race.

On the other hand, the so called negative aspects of our personality could have saved us from this fate, if they had only come to the surface if and when we were simply too comfortable to be bothered.

And so 'The Elements of Good & Evil' are going to continue until the causes of our being have been identified and converted into 'stable & predictable' social controls culminating in the creation of the cosmic fetus.

In the meantime, we may be able to connect our current status with our bio-energy in the knowledge that everything in the universe seems to be just a vibration when it comes to the ordinary matter of the universe.

That is, every atom, every part of an atom, every electron, every elementary "particle", even our thoughts and consciousness are just vibrations, in which case the 'Aura' is simply an electro-photonic vibration.

Given the vibration is always relating to the response of an object to an external excitation, the most important property of the Aura seems to be the fact that it contains information about the status of an object.

The question is "Who or what is interested in the information, for what purpose, and what is it, or are they, going to do with the information"?

At a human level, we can understand the purpose which is to inform other humans of our response to internal and external excitations or pressures of life which may have pushed us out of our 'Comfort Zone'.

In that sense, our conscious awareness of the Aura may develop in the future to the point where we can communicate on the basis of our Aura alone, which may be a lot more precise than the spoken word.

Whilst the Aura around living objects changes with time, and sometimes very quickly, (dynamic energy) the Aura around non-living object (like stones, crystals or water . . .) is essentially fixed. (constant energy)

The Aura around humans is partly composed from EM (electromagnetic) radiation spanning from microwave infrared (IR) to UV light.

The low frequency microwave and infrared part of the spectrum (body heat) seems to be related to the low levels of the functioning of our body (DNA structure, metabolism and blood circulation etc.)

On the other end of the scale, the high frequency (UV part of spectrum) is more related to our conscious activity such as thinking, creativity, intentions, sense of humour and emotions. (The Human Condition)

The colours and intensity of the aura, especially around and above the head, have very special meanings insomuch that we can actually see the other person's thoughts before we hear them expressed verbally.

And if the verbal message does not agree with what the Aura is saying, we can effectively see a lie happening right in front of our eyes since nobody can fake the Aura and the information contained therein.

The Aura is therefore our spiritual signature, and when we see a person with a bright, clean aura, we can be sure that such a person is good and spiritually advanced, even if he/she is modest and not aware of it.

And when we see a person with a grey or dark aura, we can be pretty sure the person has unclear intentions, regardless of how impressive, eloquent, educated, "good looking" or "well dressed" he/she appears.

And whilst we can imagine the power of communication associated with our conscious awareness of the meaning of the Aura, we are still largely depending on the spoken word and our body language.

In that sense, the power of communication is somewhat restricted by 'The Elements of Good & Evil', as the evil intents of the Parasite and the Predator are naturally hidden from the intended victims' consciousness.

On the other hand, the intentions of the Paradox are inclined to be more honest and open as the individual aims at a 'win-win' situation for the stakeholders, the reality of which can be seen in a loving relationship.

That is, there appears to be some kind of supernatural connection between the lovers that tends to grow or wane over time, depending on the affirmation of the original 'win-win' intent, or not, as the case may be.

By the same token, the 'win-win' relating to 'all the stakeholders' would constitute a new paradigm for the human race, whereby the behaviour of a Panacea is removing the need to hide our intentions altogether.

After all, why should we hide our thoughts and feelings from the rest of the world if they represent opportunities that are waiting to be addressed by others, if not the businesses of industry and government?

This brings us to the connection between the powers of communication and *'The study of systems which are capable of receiving, storing and processing information for the purpose of control, or Cybernetics'.*

Cybernetics has been defined in a variety of ways by a variety of people from a variety of disciplines, some of which are listed in '*The Larry Richards Reade*' as:

- "The only branch of science and math concerned with the 'Limitations' of Evolution"-Taylor Kirkland
- "The science concerned with the study of systems of any nature which are capable of receiving, storing and processing information so as to use it for control."—A. N. Kolmogorov
- "The branch of mathematics dealing with problems of control, recursiveness (a procedure that can repeat itself indefinitely) and information, focuses on forms and the patterns that connect."— Gregory Bateson
- "The art of creating equilibrium in a world of constraints and possibilities."—Ernst von Glasersfeld
- "The science and art of the understanding of understanding."— Rodney E. Donaldson
- "The way of thinking about ways of thinking of which it is one."— Larry Richards

Cybernetics is a broad field of study, the essential goal of which is to understand and define the functions and processes of systems that have goals and that participate in circular, causal chains that move from action to sensing to comparison and again to actions.

In that context, studies in cybernetics provide a means for examining the design and function of any system, including social systems such as business management for the purpose of making them more efficient and effective.

The most recent definition has been proposed by Louis Kauffman, President of the American Society for Cybernetics, "Cybernetics is the study of systems and processes that interact with themselves and produce themselves from themselves."

The word *cybernetics* was first used in the context of "the study of self-governance" by Plato in The Alcibiades to signify the governance of people and "The Pursuit of Knowledge", as illustrated below.

The Pursuit of Knowledge

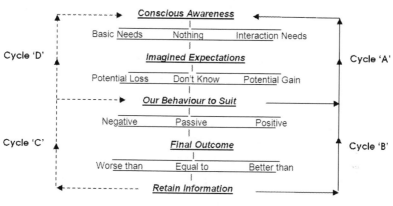

Fig.: 1.3.3

'The Pursuit of Knowledge' begins always with our 'Conscious Awareness' of our basic needs and/or our interaction needs, which may lead to our 'Imagined Expectations' of a potential gain or a loss.

If the gain is deemed worth pursuing, or the loss is worth preventing, 'Our Behaviour to Suit' our imagined expectations is now depending on our desire, ability and opportunity to achieve a desired outcome.

Whatever the case may be, 'The Pursuit of Knowledge' is now aided or hindered by our positive or negative attitude towards the situation in hand together with a subconsciously contrived body language.

And so the process (Cycle 'A') continues until we are faced with a new situation or the 'Final Outcome' can be assed with respect to its better than, equal to, or worse than, the imagined expectations or aspired goal.

The information relating to our experiences is now retained in our conscious (Cycle 'B') resulting in our improved conscious awareness and imagined expectations relating to our basic needs and interaction needs.

This brings us to Cycle 'C' and the information retained in the subconscious, the purpose of which is to assist the conscious mind by way of developing subconsciously acquired and initiated skills and habits.

In doing so, the need gratification will be dealt with by the subconscious without having to involve the conscious, (mind) that is, until the skills or habits are no longer adequate or fair, which brings us to Cycle 'D'.

On the other hand, if the skill or habit is deemed to affect the sustainability of the life form, it may be passed on to the next generation, when the genes are taking care of the pressures with an automatic reflex.

In doing so, 'The Pursuit of Knowledge' is adapting us to the environment of change and competition with an increasing array of subconsciously contrived skills and habits and unconsciously contrived reflexes.

'The Pursuit of Knowledge' begins with our conception and conscious awareness of 'Nothing', and so we 'Don't Know' what to expect as we adopt a 'Passive' behaviour to suit our perception of reality at the time.

And whilst we have no conscious awareness and expectations relating to 'our' basic needs and interaction needs, we are in tune with our mother's notions and emotions as we grow and develop in the womb.

As a consequence, if our mother has problems with respect to 'her' conscious awareness and imagined expectations, we may pick up on this and run with it until we have modified the underlying cause(s).

On the other hand, this may not take place during our life time, as the symptoms relating to our problems may be ignored, misunderstood, misdiagnosed of deferred due to a lack of funds or priority at the time.

Under the circumstances, the 'stable & predictable' deprivation or abuse of our mother's basic needs or interaction needs may be manifested in 'our' genes and thus carried over to the next generation, and so on.

This brings us to the source of our energy and emotions before, during and after our deployment of the body, whereby the SOUL takes on the role of the 'Mitochondria' during 'The Pursuit of Knowledge'.

In doing so, the accuracy of our perception is not going to affect our energy and emotions until the final outcome is compared against the imagined expectations and we are punished or rewarded for our efforts.

This, in turn, will shape our conscious awareness and imagined expectations in the future as we continue to pursue the great unknown during our childhood, adolescence, adulthood and parenthood, until we die.

The role of the 'SOUL' has never really been understood, as we can see in the phrase "Save our Souls" and similar references to the assumption that the Soul has the capacity to live on, whilst the mind is left behind.

On the other hand, there may be a connection, as the reincarnation of the mind may be determined by the 'Subordinate of the Universal Organization of Life' and its assessment of our suitability for another life.

A further misperception of reality can be seen in the frequent assumption that the human being is made up of a body and a Soul, in which case the MIND doesn't get a mention at all within the context of life.

Under the circumstances, the 'SOUL' would be responsible for the pursuit of the great unknown, in which case it would be giving itself the positive, passive and negative feelings, which is of course ridiculous.

Others are claiming that the SOUL is the SELF, in which case the SOUL is representing a schizophrenic source of intelligence that is constantly torn between the knowledge of the past and the future of mankind.

At the same time, it has the ability to 'dial up' a permanent state of happiness, which it somehow decides not to pursue in favour of a mixture of good and bad feelings for which it also has no point of reference.

After all, if it did have a point of reference, it would be going straight like an arrow to the known and measurable target of life without using the process of trial and error, in which case 'we' would not be required.

This brings us to our role as a hunter and gatherer of information, the nature of which is constantly changing our perception of reality and the good and evil associated with our situation at any moment in time.

No wonder *"The degree of our problems at any one time is proportionate to the perception of reality by one and all"*, in which case some people seem to have no problems at all, whilst others are constantly in trouble.

That is not to say one or the other is correct when it comes to their perception of reality, but rather the fact that 'We', the 'MIND', determine our physical and mental health at any one time with the help of the 'SOUL'.

In doing so, we are 'automatically' engaging in a ritual of life and death that is uncanny when it comes to the modes of behaviour and their application by the individual in the context of the creation of a cosmic foetus.

1.4   The Ritual of Life & Death

By 'Ritual', we are referring to 'The Metaphysical Aspects' of our life and 'The Modes of Behaviour', which are repeated time and again until we run out the desire, ability and/or opportunity to go on living.

Let us look at the purpose of our basic needs and our interaction needs, for which we acquire a fitness relating to our basic purpose and ultimate purpose in life, respectively, which then has to be protected.

If successful, we are now in a position to look for an application for our fitness, which is then followed up by our applying ourselves to one or the other purpose, as illustrated below under "The Ritual of Life & Death".

The Ritual of Life & Death

Stage	Modes of Behaviour	Basic Purpose	Ultimate Purpose
1	Acquire Fitness for Purpose	Need to Survive	Want to be Instructed
2	Protect Acquired Fitness	Need to be Safe	Want to be Consulted
3	Find Application for Fitness	Need to Belong	Want to be Included
4	Apply Fitness to Purpose	Need to be Valued	Want to be Delegated
5	Consider Greater Fitness	Need to be Fulfilled	Want to be Left Alone

Fig.: 1.4.1

The ritual begins with our predetermined modes of behaviour at the time of our conception in the womb, where the forces of Nature provide a secure environment without us having to worry about anything whatsoever.

From thereon, the ritual is bound to become increasingly self-determined as we grow and develop from the time of our birth to the time of our natural death, the duration of which may vary between individuals and nations.

That is, whilst everything in life and death here on earth has a purpose, the duration of our life depends entirely on our accrued physical and mental capacity for dealing with the internal and external pressures.

As a consequence, some may live longer than others, the reason for which lies in their need to a) represent the physiological or psychological problems of the past, or b) continue with the pursuit of the great unknown.

As to the latter, the element of competition can be seen at stage 4, which may be effected in the physical dimension through the pursuit of sex, and the metaphysical dimension through the pursuit of science.

This brings us to the uniqueness of our bodies and minds and our need to specialize in the pursuit of knowledge, the reality of which is reflected in the natural distribution of our physical and mental fitness characteristics.

The phenomenon is not unlike the natural distribution of our behaviour relating to 'The Forces of Nature & Nurture' or comfort zone, where the limits are representing our fitness for dealing with the great unknown.

And whilst the distribution of our physical fitness and limits is a reflection of our need to survive here on earth, our metaphysical fitness and limits is reflecting our mental capacity and need to survive in the universe.

By the same token, the need for our physical fitness and specialization is bound to decrease over time as our metaphysical fitness is increasing to the point where we have attained a worldwide state of 'Mind over Matter'.

If we apply the ritual to 'The Survival of the Fittest', then stage one starts with the fitness of our mother's eggs which have to be protected until they are mature and ready to be expelled into the fallopian tube.

In doing so, the mature egg is hoping to find an application for its fitness in the form of a male sperm resulting in its fertilization and application of its fitness to the creation of a human foetus in the womb.

All going well, the human foetus will consider a greater fitness by way of its expulsion from the womb, upon which the ritual starts all over again during our childhood, adolescence, adulthood and parenthood.

This brings us to our metaphysical dimension and fitness for a higher purpose than our survival on the planet earth, the reality of which is based on our interaction needs, as we can see in our feelings whenever:

1. We are being instructed in the use of our car by a backseat driver and we are starting to lose our cool.
2. We are in a queue and someone is pushing in without consulting us with respect to our permission to do so.
3. We are expected to achieve a seemingly impossible target without having been included in the decision making.
4. We are being delegated the responsibility for the achievement of an objective without having been given the means.

5. We are being told by our parents to embark on a career that should have been left to us and our particular aspirations in life.

Why should we get upset about such a small issue, when it would be much easier to 'shut up and do as we are told', and at the same time save us a lot of heartache and stresses that may even kill us and/or others?

At the same time, if the problem relating to our interaction needs is sufficiently widespread or severe, the community may get up in arms and appeal to the businesses of industry and/or government, as the case may be.

In the process, our interaction needs may override our basic need to survive, as we can see when we are being instructed by the boss with words like "Do as you are bloody told", which may cause us to swear at him.

In doing so, we may get the sack and end up without an income to support the wife and four kids, or pay the mortgage and all the other bills, in which case we may rethink our priorities and apologize to the boss.

On the other hand, we may stand our ground as we are prepared to sacrifice our basic needs for the sake of our interaction needs, which may sound like a stupid thing to do, but then again, somebody has to do it.

At the same time, we would have done our best to berate the image of the business and condemn its practices in our social circles and anywhere else whenever we were asked the question of 'How are you going?'

The scenario is representing 'The Battle of Nature & Nurture', which is bound to affect the earnings, security, image, distinction and/or growth of the business, as illustrated below under "The Ritual of Industry".

The Ritual of Industry

Stage	Modes of Behaviour	Business Needs	Stakeholders
1.	Acquire Fitness for Purpose	Earnings	Customer
2.	Protect the Acquired Fitness	Security	Supplier
3.	Find Application for Fitness	Image	Employee
4.	Apply Fitness to Purpose	Distinction	Shareholder
5.	Consider Greater Fitness	Growth	Community

Fig.: 1.4.2

The first business of industry would have sprung into life when a 'gifted' individual created a product or a service for which there was an 'unstable but predictable' demand within the community at large.

As the demand increased, the business would have sought a supplier or two for its raw materials, components, deliveries and similar aspects relating to the business process so as to protect is acquired fitness.

As the business became profitable, the originator or owner would have employed unskilled people to do the menial work, whilst he concentrated on the development of an image for the business in the market place.

The ongoing success of the business would have encouraged other people to invest their money in the business, which allowed it to focus on the research and development of new and exciting products and services.

And so the businesses of industry were applying their fitness to 'Our Ultimate Purpose in Life' as they were pursuing the great unknown so as to advance the human race, using the process of trial and error.

As to the latter, many a business of industry is struggling whilst it is addressing its obvious 'Need to Change' its image in the light of the potential losses having become actual losses on the financial 'Bottom Line'.

In order to deal with the situation, some businesses adopted a 'participative management' style, where employees have a strong decision-making role and a cooperative relationship with the management team.

At the same time there are Advantages and Disadvantages associated with Participative Management, as we can see in the findings of the 'Management Study Guide', whereby:

<u>The Advantages of Participative Management</u>

The participative approach to management increases the stake or ownership of employees. But there is more to it. The following points elucidate the same.

- <u>Increase in Productivity</u>: An increased say in decision making means that there is a strong feeling of association now. The employee now assumes responsibility and takes charges. There is lesser new or delegation or supervision from the manager. Working hours may get stretched on their own without any compulsion or force from the management. All this leads to increased productivity.

- <u>Job Satisfaction</u>: In lots or organizations that employ participative management, most of the employees are satisfied with their jobs and the level of satisfaction id very high. This is specially when people see their suggestions and recommendations being implemented or put to practice. Psychologically, this tells the individual employee that, 'he too has a say in decision making and that he too is an integral component of the organization and not a mere worker'.

- <u>Motivation</u>: Increased productivity and job satisfaction cannot exist unless there is a high level of motivation in the employee. The vice versa also holds true! Decentralized decision making means that everyone has a say and everyone is important.

- <u>Improved Quality</u>: Since the inputs or feedback comes from people who are part of the processes at the lowest or execution level. This means that even the minutest details are taken care of and reported. No flaw or loophole goes unreported. Quality control is thus begins and is ensured at the lowest level.

- <u>Reduced Costs</u>: There is a lesser need of supervision and more emphasis is laid on widening of skills, self management. This and quality control means that the costs are controlled automatically.

<u>The Disadvantages of Participative Management</u>

There is a flip side to everything; participative management stands no exception to it. Whereas this style of leadership or decision making leads to better participation of all the employees, there are undoubtedly some disadvantages too.

- <u>Decision making slows down:</u> Participative management stands for increased participation and when there are many people involved in decision making, the process definitely slows down. Inputs and feedback starts pouring from each side. It takes time to verify the accuracy of measurements which means that decision making will be slowed down.
- <u>Security Issue:</u> The security issue in participative management also arises from the fact that since early stages too many people are known to lots of facts and information. This information may transform into critical information in the later stages. There is thus a greater apprehension of information being leaked out.

The advantages seem to outnumber the disadvantages; this however is no assurance that one should blindly adopt it, as every organization is different, and therefore the culture and the human resources, in which case a deep understanding of both is required in order to ascertain a decision making style and adopt the same.

Another source is making the following observation:

"Our company involves everyone from the clerks in the mailroom to the president in decisions." Sounds like a dream come true, doesn't it? Everyone's opinion counts. No one's ideas are ignored just because of title (or lack thereof). A truly democratic process that makes people feel needed—it empowers them.

That is until you find that your staffers are starting to challenge all your ideas, or perhaps you find that the staff is more concerned with voicing its opinion and frustrations with management than in getting work done.

Then there are all those ideas that, however well-meaning, are off the mark, impractical, or just plain stupid, and so begin to realize that participative management wasn't what Mae West had in mind when she said that "too much of a good thing is wonderful."

As it stands, the businesses of industry are still searching for the ultimate management system, the key to which lies in the simple fact that every business represents a social organ, the survival of which is not unlike the human organs.

That is, the human organs are depending on the support of the cells when it comes to the aspirations of the 'Metaphysical Intelligence for the Notional Deployment' of the body, or MIND, for short.

In that context, the single-minded focus on the earnings and possibly the security of the business is not going to lead to its sustainability in the long term, the reality of which is becoming more obvious every day.

This brings us to the community at large and its desire, ability and opportunity to participate in the business of government, as illustrated below under "The Ritual of Government".

The Ritual of Government

Stage	Modes of Behaviour	Power	Management Style
1.	Acquire Fitness for Purpose	Mythology	Instruct Stakeholders
2.	Protect the Acquired Fitness	Military	Consult Stakeholders
3.	Find Application for Fitness	Majority	Include Stakeholders
4.	Apply Fitness to Purpose	Morality	Delegate Stakeholders
5.	Consider Greater Fitness	Mentality	Leave Stakeholders Alone

Fig.: 1.4.3

As to the growth and development of our mental capacity, the evidence can be seen in the powers of Mythology and the Military and their replacement by the powers of the Majority, or democratic system and Paradox.

And whilst the democratic system or social Paradox "sees only to the needs of some of its stakeholders", the minority groups and the hereditary classes may or may not be prepared to go along with the Majority rule.

And so the element of fairness continues to rear its ugly head until the needs and expectations of 'all' the stakeholders are being addressed by the prevailing businesses of industry and government.

Whilst this may lead to the interim resurgence of some religions, this is not going to affect the separation of church and state, or growing distance in the relationship between organized religion and the nation state.

Although the concept of separation has been adopted in a number of countries, there are varying degrees of separation depending on the applicable legal structures and prevalent views toward the proper role of religion in society.

While a country's policy may be to have a definite distinction in church and state, there may be an "arm's length" distant relationship in which the two entities interact as independent organizations.

A similar but typically stricter principle of neutrality has been applied in France and Turkey, while some socially secularized countries such as Denmark and the United Kingdom have maintained constitutional recognition of an official state religion.

A similar separation of the Military and state, or growing distance in the relationship between organized military or police intervention and the nation state is finding its way into our current policies and legal structures.

Huntington (1957), in a study based primarily on the history of the military in Western societies, elaborated what was widely accepted as the liberal democratic model of civil-military interaction when he stated that:

"The principal responsibility of the military officer is to the state', as politics is beyond the scope of military competence, and the participation of military officers in politics undermines their professionalism.

The military officer must therefore remain neutral politically, whilst the area of military science is subordinate to, and yet independent of, the area of politics, where the military profession exists to serve the state and the superior political wisdom of the statesman must be accepted as a fact."

This brings us to 'The Evolution of Government Policy on Widening Participation' and Paul Greenbank who published an article first published online: 24 March 2006

This article examines the evolution of government policy in England as it traces government policy on widening participation in relation to social class from 1963 through to 'The Future of Higher Education' (2003)

The article concludes that there is a lack of participation in policy formulation by certain key groups and, although the widening participation policy has generally progressed, it has done so within an <u>overly bureaucratic system of control</u> that fails to give higher education institutions the autonomy they need.

There are also occasions when aspects of policy seem to be taking backward steps, while the government adopts rhetoric on strategic rationality and a piecemeal approach that lacks cohesive and evidence-based rationale.

This reminds us of Wallace B. Donham, Harvard Business School's second dean who noted that *"the world's problems would not be solved through governmental or police intervention, but from within on a higher ethical plane".*

The observation is supported by the philosopher Socrates who claimed some 450 years B.C. that *"the problems of this world will not diminish until politicians become philosophers, and philosophers become politicians.*

The significance of that statement lies in the meaning of the word philosophy representing *"The study and analysis of the principles underlying thought, conduct, knowledge and the nature of the universe."*

Hence, if the voters want philosophy in politics and the desire becomes part of their political striving, philosophers will offer themselves to lead the community to "The Higher Ethical Plane", as illustrated below.

The Higher Ethical Plane

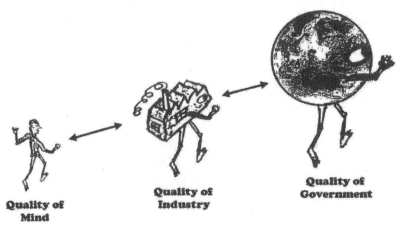

Quality of Mind   **Quality of Industry**   **Quality of Government**

Fig.: 1.4.4

In that context, *"the world's problems would not be solved through governmental or police intervention"* but rather through our conscious awareness of who we are as an individual and what we are doing on this planet

The illustration portrays the powers of Morality, which begin with the individual stakeholders and their perception of reality relating to the businesses of industry and government representing a Panacea.

In that sense, the concept of a Panacea is based on a management system where problems are not just solved as they emerge to our consciousness, but rather prevented from occurring in the first place.

In order to do so, we need to understand the principles underlying thought, conduct, knowledge and the nature of the universe, (laws of metaphysics) the conscious awareness of which begins with:

a) The seekers of knowledge who are 'constructively discontent' with the scientific communities and/or belief systems and their answers to 'Our Ultimate Purpose in Life', which is leaving them in a moral vacuum.

b) The education, training and consulting facilities who are ultimately responsible for shaping the minds of the up and coming generations with respect to their desire and ability to create a better world for all mankind.

c) The businesses of industry which are left to the process of trial and error when it comes to their obligations as a human organization and commitment to the needs and expectations of the stakeholders, one and all.

We can compare the concept to the human body and the relationship between the cells, the organs and the mind, whereby potential problems are prevented from occurring until we reach the predetermined limits.

And so the mind is informed with an internal pressure reflecting the importance of the need and the nature of the deprivation, in the hope that it might address the situation and thus prevent a potential problem.

In the meantime, the cells and organs are prepared to give their one and all to the aims and objectives of the human mind culminating in 'Our Ultimate Purpose in Life', in which lies the key to 'The Higher Ethical Plane'.

And whilst none of the cells and organs are designed to behave in the manner of a Parasite, a Predator or a Paradox, the body is not immune to the external Parasites, Predators and Paradoxes of this world.

This brings us back to the 'Quality of Industry' and its comparison to a Panacea, in which case none of the stakeholders are inclined to behave in the manner of a Parasite, a Predator or a Paradox to the business.

At the same time, the businesses of industry are not immune to the external Parasites, Predators and Paradoxes unless the businesses of government adopt the behaviour of a Panacea or 'Quality of Government.

In doing so, there would be no further need for charity organizations and philanthropists, as the needs and expectations of the community are catered for by the businesses of industry and government, and vice versa.

The phenomenon is obviously associated with the creation of a cosmic foetus which, unlike the predetermined growth and development of the human foetus, is based on the self-determination of the mind.

In that context, there is a connection between the physical body and the role of the businesses of industry, as there is a connection between the metaphysical mind and the businesses of government.

As to the first, the connection to the business of industry is based on 'The Process of Natural Selection', whereby the lack of adequacy is reflected in the 4,200 genes representing the diseases of the body.

By the same token, the totality of the gene pool is reflecting the growth and development of the cosmic fetus, in which case the fitness for purpose is transmitted between individuals nationally and internationally.

In other words, it is not good enough for one group of people, nation or part of the world to become a 'super race' or genetically advanced human species unless the concept is extended to the rest of the world.

As it stands, we still have a long way to go before the 'stable & predictable' adequacy of our skills and habits is manifested in our genes to the point where we do not have any more genetically inherited diseases.

This brings us to the connection between the metaphysical mind and the businesses of government, the reality of which is reflected in our cosmic connection and 'The Process of Supernatural Selection'.

1.5   The Cosmic Connection

Let us begin with the laws of physics and our cosmic connection to the chemical elements which are all around us, like the composition of the earth and the chemistry that governs its biology rooted in these elements.

The elements have their origins in cosmic events, whereby different elements come from a variety of different events that take place in the universe, like the hydrogen was formed in the moments after the Big Bang.

Similarly, carbon (the basis for all terrestrial life) was formed in small stars, whereas elements of lower abundance in living organisms but essential to our biology, such as calcium and iron, were formed in large stars.

Heavier elements important to our environment, such as gold, were formed in the explosive power of supernovae, whereby light, the elements used in our modern technology, was formed via cosmic rays.

The solar nebula from which our solar system was formed was seeded with these elements, and they were present at the earth's formation, in which case our very existence is connected to these elements.

At the same time, they do not tell us anything about the evolution of life and the emergence of modern man, nor do they tell us anything about the 'Grand Order of Design' and its connection to 'The Human Condition'.

This brings us to 'Our Ultimate Purpose in Life' and 'The Process of Supernatural Selection' representing the growth and development of the human mind, as illustrated below under "The Cosmic Connection".

The Cosmic Connection

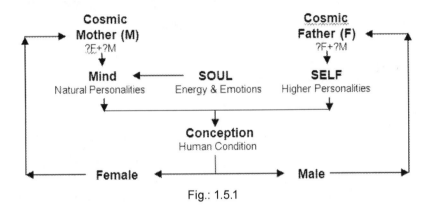

Fig.: 1.5.1

The illustration portrays the forces of Nature and Nurture, where the satisfaction of our basic needs is reflected in the phenomenon of our 'Natural Personalities', and the interaction needs in our 'Higher Personalities'.

Note: The topic of our personalities will be discussed in detail in Part 2 'The Human Condition'.

'The Cosmic Connection' is reflecting 'The Nature of the Universe', in which case the constant energy represents our cosmic mother and 'Need to Change' versus the dynamic energy as our cosmic father and 'Want to Compete'.

In that context, 'The Cosmic Connection' is not dissimilar to our human connection relating to our parents and their parents, etc. the origin of which can be traced right back to the beginning of life on earth.

'The Cosmic Connection' can also be found in the realms of psychology in the form of a Type A and Type B personality theory that describes two common, contrasting personality types:

A—the high-strung and B—the easy-going that could either raise (A)'s, or lower (B)'s, chances of developing coronary heart disease, which was originally published in the 1950s.

Though it has been widely controversial in the scientific and medical communities since its publication, the theory has nonetheless persisted, both in the form of pop psychology and in the general lexicon of psychology.

The 8.5 year research by cardiologists Meyer Friedman and Ray Rosenman had a significant effect on the way in which psychologists look at how an individual's mental state affects his or her physical health.

Under the circumstances, the Type A and Type B personalities are bound to be associated with the 'Seeker of Eternal Life and Fulfilment' (SELF), which began with the emergence of modern man some 200,000 years ago.

By the same token, we can assume a connection between 'The Higher Personalities' and 'Our Ultimate Purpose in Life', the reality of which is played out in the physical and metaphysical dimension.

As to the latter, the contrast between the easy going and the high strung personality types may be also be connected with the phenomenon of "The Left & Right Brain Functions", respectively, as illustrated below.

The Left & Right Brain Functions

LEFT BRAIN FUNCTIONS	RIGHT BRAIN FUNCTIONS
uses logic	uses feeling
detail oriented	big picture oriented
facts rule	imagination rules
words and language	symbols and images
present and past	present and future
math and science	philosophy & religion
can comprehend	can "get it" (i.e. meaning)
knowing	believes
acknowledges	appreciates
order/pattern perception	spatial perception
knows object name	knows object function
reality based	fantasy based
forms strategies	presents possibilities
practical	impetuous
safe	risk taking

Fig.: 1.5.2

The illustration is portraying 'The Battle of Nature & Nurture', whereby the left brain is focusing on the knowledge of the present and past, whereas the right brain is focusing on the present and the future.

Each of these 'brains' has an outer layer of grey matter called the cerebral cortex that is supported by an inner layer of white matter. In eutherian or placental mammals (but not in non-eutherian mammals such as marsupials, nor in other vertebrates), the brains are linked by the corpus callosum.

Whilst the brains or 'hemispheres' are roughly mirror images of each other, with only subtle differences, the architecture, types of cells, types of neurotransmitters and receptor subtypes are markedly asymmetrical between the two hemispheres.

However, while some of these hemispheric distribution differences are consistent across human beings, or even across some species, many observable distribution differences vary from individual to individual within a given species.

This takes us to the question of "How do male and female minds differ in their development and structure?" as in most cases, female brains mature earlier than males, some which is due to the myelination of the brain or coating, which allows electrical impulses to travel down a nerve fast and efficiently.

Myelination continues in all brains into the early twenties, but in young women it is complete earlier than in young men, almost twelve-eighteen months earlier. Because of this, females, for instance, can acquire their complex verbal skills as much as a year earlier than males.

Thus, quite often, a female will learn to read faster and achieve a larger vocabulary than her male peers, and she may speak with better grammar, which seems to continue throughout development, whereby female brains tend to develop quicker than male brains.

Another structural difference, and perhaps the most striking, is the corpus callosum, the bundle of nerves that connects emotion and cognition which is up to 20% larger in females than in males, giving females better decision making and sensory processing skills.

Considering all learning must connect emotion and cognition, this difference in size means that females have better verbal abilities and rely heavily on verbal communication, whilst males tend to rely heavily on nonverbal communication and are less likely to verbalize feelings.

The current research suggests that sixty-seven per cent of males throughout their life are visual learners. This learning style has immense ramifications in our present culture, which relies so heavily on talk, conversation and words.

Males and females also have a differing amount of most of the brain chemicals. Perhaps the most telling difference is in how much serotonin each brain secretes, whereby the male brain secretes less than the female, thus making males impulsive in general, as well as fidgety.

Oxtocin is another one of the brain chemicals that, being more constantly stimulated in females, make the female capable of quick and immediate empathic responses to others' pain and needs.

And whilst we can associate the brain chemicals and the development and structure of the brain with the physical aspects of life, we are nevertheless left in the dark when it comes to our metaphysical aspects.

That is, the creation and secretion of the chemicals is not a function of the male or female brain, but rather a function of the SOUL in response to the male's or female's perception of reality and purpose in life.

The situation is not unlike our investigation of the car and the mechanics of the drive train from the motor to the wheels, without understanding the reason for the car and the various controls relating to its application.

And so we come to the misperception of reality that the carburettor or fuel injection is the stuff that motivates the car, which somehow evolved mysteriously over a century or so for no reason other than to please God.

This brings us to the controversial question of our mental gender predisposition beyond the physical 'X + X' (female) and 'X + Y' (male) chromosomes in line with 'The Process of Supernatural Selection'.

That is, apart from our inherited genes and the associated physiological predisposition, our mind is also predisposed with respect to our desire to live our live as a male or a female member of the community.

The mental gender predisposition is reflecting the forces of Nature or our Cosmic Mother, whereby the 'Natural Personalities' are designed to facilitate 'The Survival of the Fittest' animals and human beings.

The phenomenon is supported by the scientific finding that certain parts of the human brain are differently sized in the male and female genders, whereby the male brain is slightly larger than the female brain.

The study also found that certain parts of the frontal lobe of the brain responsible for problem-solving and decision-making and the limbic cortex responsible for regulating emotions were larger in women.

On the other hand, men have about 6.5 times more gray matter than women who have about 10 times more white matter than men do, which may account for some of the differences in how men and women think.

At the same time, it does not account for the notions and emotions associated with the role of the father and the mother, which are essentially different when it comes to 'The Survival of the Fittest' here on earth.

The phenomenon would explain the gender confusion relating to a female body and a male mind, and vice versa, whereby the homosexual tendency may be related to a mismatch or confusion of the human minds.

In the case of a mismatch, we can imagine a female mind growing up in a male body, and vice versa, in which case the individual is increasingly caught between the pressures from within and/or without.

And whilst the current scientific and medical understanding is that sexual orientation is not a choice, but rather a complex interplay of biological and environmental factors, this is not explaining the whole story.

There are those who still hold the view that homosexual activity is "unnatural" or "dysfunctional", even though research has shown that homosexuality is a normal and natural variation in human sexuality.

Furthermore, most people experience little or no sense of choice about their sexuality, and there is also insufficient evidence to support the use of psychological interventions to change sexual orientation.

However, prejudice and discrimination against homosexuals and bisexuals have been shown to cause significant psychological harm, and are especially damaging to children who are homosexual or bisexual.

This brings us to the businesses of government and "The Evolution of Power", the purpose of which is ultimately associated with the expansion of populations, cities, warfare and nations, as illustrated below.

The Evolution of Power

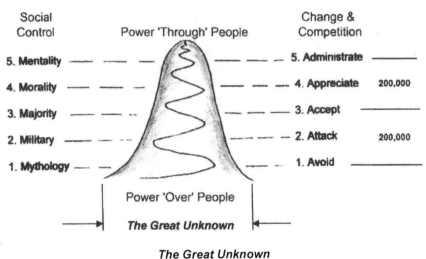

Power 'Over' People

The Great Unknown

The Great Unknown

Fig.: 1.5.3

The illustration is portraying our journey towards the pinnacle of our existence here on earth and the evolution of the social controls from a power 'over' people concept to a power 'through' people concept.

'The Evolution of Power' is directly associated with the emerging interest in 'The Great Unknown' which began some 200,000 years ago with the emergence of modern man, and is now more important than ever.

The evolution of the social controls began with the powers of Mythology, where the power was based on the proposition of an 'Almighty' source of power and the avoidance of any kind of change and competition.

In doing so, the power 'over' people concept managed to provide a 'stable & predictable' environment for the community at large, which was basically essential for the creation of the businesses of industry.

The powers of Mythology represent the first stage in the creation of a cosmic foetus, as we can see in the frantic multiplication of the human race that now needed to be protected by the powers of the Military.

In order to do so, the Military resorted to a strategy of attacking any change and competition to the point where the world was slowly coming together under the banner of one military might and persuasion or another.

Much of what we know of ancient history these days is the history of militaries relating to their conquests, their movements and their technological innovations, and there are many good reasons for this.

That is, kingdoms and empires with central units of control could only be maintained through military force, as the limited agricultural ability could not support large communities, and so fighting was common place.

Notable militaries in the ancient world include the Egyptians, Babylonians, Persians, Ancient Greeks, Indians, Early Imperial Chinese, Xiongnu Confederation, Ancient Romans, and Carthaginians.

The fertile crescent of Mesopotamia was the centre of several prehistoric conquests, where. Mesopotamia was conquered by the Sumerians, Akkadians, Babylonians, Assyrians and Persians, whilst Iranians were the first nation to introduce cavalry into their army.

Egypt began growing as an ancient power, but eventually fell to the Libyans, Nubians, Assyrians, Persians, Greeks, Romans, Byzantines and Arabs.

Alexander the Great invaded North-western India and defeated King Porus in the Battle of the Hydaspes River, which was soon re-conquered by Chandragupta Maurya after defeating the Macedonians and Seleucids.

He also went on to conquer the Nanda Empire and unify Northern India, whilst most of Southern Asia was unified under his grandson Ashoka the Great after the Kalinga War, though the empire collapsed not long after his reign.

In China, the Shang Dynasty and Zhou Dynasty had risen and collapsed, which led to a Warring States period in which several states continued to fight with each other over territory, whilst philosopher-strategists such as Confucius and Sun Tzu wrote various manuscripts on ancient warfare and international diplomacy.

The concept of warfare continued throughout the medieval period and, as weapons—particularly small arms—became easier to use, countries began to abandon a complete reliance on professional soldiers in favour of conscription.

Conscription was employed in industrial warfare to increase the number of soldiers that were available for combat, and it was used by Napoleon Bonaparte in the Napoleonic Wars.

Total war was used in industrial warfare, the objective being to prevent the opposing nation to engage in war, which is referred to by William Tecumseh Sherman's "March to the Sea" and Philip Sheridan's burning of the Shenandoah Valley.

In modern times, war has evolved from an activity steeped in tradition to a scientific enterprise, where success is valued above the methods and the notion of total war is the extreme of this trend.

And whilst militaries have developed technological advances rivalling the scientific accomplishments of any other field of study, it should be noted that modern militaries benefit in the development of these technologies under the funding of the public, the leadership of national governments, and often in cooperation with large civilian groups, such as the General Dynamics and Lockheed Martin corporations, in the United States.

And as for the phenomenon of "total war", it may be argued that it is not an exclusive practice of modern militaries, but in the tradition of genocidal conflict that marks the practice of tribal warfare to this day.

What distinguishes the modern military from those previous is not their willingness to prevail in conflict by any method, but rather the technological variety of tools and methods available to modern battlefield commanders, from submarines to satellites and nuclear warheads.

World War I was sparked by the assassination of Archduke Franz Ferdinand, leading to the mobilization of Austria and Serbia, where the Germans joined the Austrians to form the Central powers, whilst the French, British, and Russians formed the Allied powers.

World War II erupted after Germany's invasion of Poland, thus forcing Britain and France to declare war on Germany, upon which Germany quickly defeated France and Belgium, which was later aided by Italy.

Meanwhile, Japan, who had already been at war with the Chinese since 1937, had launched a surprise attack on Pearl Harbor, which led to the United States joining the Allied powers.

In Europe, the Allies opened three fronts; in the west after securing Normandy; in the east, aiding the Soviet Union; and in the south, through Italy which forced Germany eventually to surrender, upon which the Allies turned and focused troops to do island hopping.

The dropping of the atom bombs on Hiroshima and Nagasaki led to the surrender of Japan and the end of the Second World War, which subsequently led to the worsening of relationships between wartime Allies.

As it stands, the Defence Spending Budgets of the top nations are around $690 billion for the United State, $130 billion for China, $64 billion for France, $57 for the United Kingdom followed by Japan at $54 billion all the way down to $1 billion for Croatia.

As a percentage of the total budget for the year, the United States is spending some 23% on defence, followed by China with 8% and Russia with 3.5%, whilst the defence budget of the world is about $1.85 trillion US.

And to think there is really no need for any nation to defend itself against any other, the Notion of which goes back to the invention of agriculture, the creation of nations and the emergence of mass religion.

In doing so, the cost of living continued to rise to the point where *"the degree of our problems at any one time is proportionate to the perception of reality by one and all"*, which brings us to the Majority rule.

To be specific, the community at large got tired of being treated with contempt by the ruling classes, and so they rebelled on mass in an attempt to replace the system of government with a democratic system.

And whilst the democratic system of government by the people directly or by representative seemed fair to the greater Majority of people, it was only tolerating minority groups and ignoring hereditary classes.

At the same time, the democratic system of government was accepting the elements of change and competition, which gave the minority groups and the hereditary classes a chance to make their mark.

The history of democracy traces back from classical Athens in the 6th century B.C. to the present day, where democracy is a political system in which all the members of the society have an equal share of formal political power.

Note: In modern representative democracy, this formal equality is embodied primarily in the right to vote.

Although it is generally believed that the concepts of democracy and constitution were created in one particular place and time—identified as Ancient Athens circa 508 BCE—there is evidence to suggest that democratic forms of government, in a broad sense, may have existed in several areas of the world well before the turn of the 5th century.

Within that broad sense it is plausible to assume that democracy in one form or another arises naturally in any well-bonded group, such as a tribe and tribalism or *primitive democracy.*

A *primitive democracy* is identified in small communities or villages when the following take place: face-to-face discussion in the village council or a headman whose decisions are supported by village elders or other cooperative modes of government.

Nevertheless, on a larger scale sharper contrasts arise when the village and the city are examined as political communities where, in urban governments, all other forms of rule—monarchy, tyranny, aristocracy, and oligarchy—have flourished.

Athens is regarded as the birthplace of democracy and it is considered an important reference point of democracy which emerged in the 7th century BCE, like many other cities, with a dominating powerful aristocracy.

However, this domination led to exploitation causing significant economic, political, and social problems which were enhanced early in the sixth century and as *"the many were enslaved to few, the people rose against the notables".*

At the same period in the Greek world many traditional aristocracies were disrupted by popular revolutions, like Sparta in the second half of the 7th century BCE, as Sparta's constitutional reforms by Lycurgus introduced a hoplite state and showed how inherited governments can be changed and lead to military victory.

After a period of unrest between the rich and the poor, the Athenians of all classes turned to Solon for acting as a mediator between rival factions which led to their reaching a generally satisfactory solution.

Democracy has come a long way since then, as we are now relatively free to do as we wish, as long as we are not interfering with the rights of others and their desire to do the same, most of which has nothing to do with 'The Survival of the Fittest'.

In fact, if the truth be known, we are collectively insisting on the right to kill ourselves and, as long as this is not too fast and too furious, nobody is going to object, as this is simply part of 'The Human Condition'.

In that context, 'The Evolution of Power' supports the dichotomy of 'The Quantity of Life' and 'The Quality of Life', as we can see in the powers of Mythology as they urge the followers to "go forth and multiply'.

In this day and age, we seem to have enough people, (or too many) and so our focus is on 'The Quality of Life', as we can see in the consumerism and competition between the businesses of industry and government.

PART 2.0

THE HUMAN CONDITION

2.1   The Battle of Nature & Nurture

'Our Ultimate Purpose in Life' is a reversal of our basic purpose, as the predatory method of survival and focus on the distant past is now joined by an additional focus on the near and the distant future.

In the process, the principles underlying thought, conduct, knowledge and the nature of the universe apply now to the businesses of industry and government, as illustrated below under "The Battle of Nature & Nurture".

The Battle of Nature & Nurture

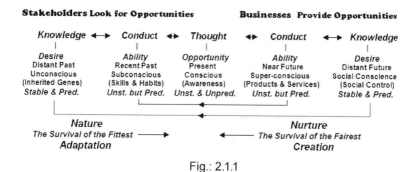

Fig.: 2.1.1

'The Battle of Nature & Nurture' explains our transition from a dependency on Nature to a dependency on the businesses of industry and government to the point where we are now living in a 'consumer society'.

Note: "*The term of 'consumer society' applies to any community in which the buying and selling of goods and services is promoted through mass media and representing the dominant economic activity*".

'The Battle of Nature & Nurture' is essentially based on the individual's perception of an opportunity relating to 'The Survival of the Fairest' versus 'The Survival of the Fittest', whereby the:

a) 'Desire + Ability + Opportunity = The Behaviour to Suit 'The Survival of the Fittest'

b) 'Opportunity + Ability + Desire = The Behaviour to Suit 'The Survival of the Fairest'

In that context, the individual may behave like an 'Animal' if it is not given the 'Opportunity' to grow and develop in the context of its mental capacity, in which case 'The Survival of the Fittest' becomes predominant.

On the other hand, if the individual is given the 'Opportunity' to grow, 'The Survival of the Fairest' is bound to become predominant, upon which the businesses of industry become the key to its 'Ability' to do so.

This brings us to the businesses of government and their powers of persuasion relating to the individual's 'Desire' to contribute towards the advancement of the human race and the associated 'Social Conscience'.

As a consequence, if the 'social controls' are deemed as 'unfair', the individual will revert back to 'The Survival of the Fittest', in which case the 'social conscience' is bound to become one of 'lawlessness'.

As it stands, we are increasingly torn between the knowledge of the distant and recent past or 'The Survival of the Fittest', and the knowledge of the near and distant future relating to 'The Survival of the Fairest'.

In doing so, our basic survival is no longer a priority when it comes to our pursuit of the great unknown, as we are inclined to abuse our bodies and minds until we find the limits relating to our physiological comfort zone.

At the same time, the entire world is on the verge of becoming a consumer society, whereby the actions of the businesses of industry and government affect, or can be affected by, any other organization or nation.

The concept began with the fertilization of the cosmic egg and the emergence of the 'super-conscious' wanting to create 'unstable but predictable' products and services for which there was a demand in the near future.

Note: *The super conscious contains within itself the possibility as well as the probability of creating anything and everything that can be conceived by the conscious mind . . . The possibilities are "Infinite".*

This is followed by a fifth level of intelligence in the form of the social conscience, the purpose of which was to create 'stable & predictable' social controls for which there was a need in the distant future.

Note: A 'Social Conscience' represents *"A sense of responsibility towards social injustice and problems in the belief that there is an intimate bond among individuals that benefits all of us collectively".*

By the same token, if the products and/or services were not adequate and/or the social controls were not fair, the stakeholders would inform the community in no uncertain terms with respect to the problem.

This brings us to the uniqueness of our bodies and minds and the associated natural distribution of our fitness characteristics relating to 'The Survival of the Fittest' and 'The Survival of the Fairest'.

The phenomenon is like our behaviour relating to the limits of our comfort zone, as shown under 'The Forces of Nature & Nurture', with the exception that we are now referring to 'Our Ultimate Purpose in Life'.

Under the circumstances, if there is a moderate shift in the limits of our comfort zone like a change in the natural environment or the social environment, the majority of bodies or minds will remain comfortable.

As to the plight of the unfortunate symptom bearers, their role is to attract the businesses of industry and government who may then see fit to research and develop new products and services and social controls.

But the again, they may not, as we know only too well whenever we express our needs and expectations from the respective businesses, only to find out that 'We' do not represent a 'commercial opportunity'.

As a consequence, we may become an integral part of the problem or the solution, as we succumb to the symptoms, or seek to identify and modify the root causes and thus advance the human race, respectively.

As to the distribution of our mental fitness relating to 'Our Ultimate Purpose in Life', the reality can be seen in the intelligence quotient, or IQ, which is a score derived from one of several standardized tests designed to assess intelligence.

The abbreviation "IQ" comes from the German term *Intelligenz-Quotient*, which was originally coined by the psychologist William Stern.

When current IQ tests are developed, the median or average raw score of the sample is defined as IQ 100 and scores each standard deviation (SD) up or down are defined as 15 IQ points greater or less, although this was not always so historically.

By this definition, approximately 95 percent of the population scores an IQ between 70 and 130, which is within two standard deviations of the median.

IQ scores have been shown to be associated with such factors as morbidity and parental social status and, to a substantial degree, biological parental IQ.

While the heritability of IQ has been investigated for nearly a century, there is still debate about the significance of heritability estimates and the mechanisms of inheritance.

Whilst IQ scores are used as predictors of educational achievement, special needs, job performance and income., they are also used to study IQ distributions in populations and the correlations between IQ and other variables.

Raw scores on IQ tests for many populations have been rising at an average rate that scales to three IQ points per decade since the early 20th century, a phenomenon called the Flynn effect.

In that context, it seems like the increase in our IQ is taking us closer to the pinnacle of our existence on earth, the next stage of which (or social model of behaviour) is associated with the behaviour of a Panacea.

That is, instead of focusing only on the problems so as to stop them from recurring, we are going to focus on the monitoring of the root causes so as to prevent the problems from occurring in the first place.

This brings us back to the 'Cost of Living' which, unlike the 'Cost of Commuting', is far more complex, as it involves everything associated with life, as illustrated below under "The Personal Cycle of Life & Death".

The Personal Cycle of Life & Death

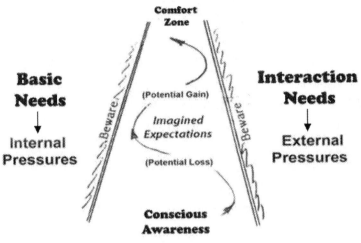

Fig.: 2.1.2

That is, much of our hard earned money is spent on the acquisition of products, services and social controls so as to maintain our comfort zone, or to address the myriad of diseases of the body and the mind.

The illustration portrays the connection between our comfort zone and our conscious awareness of the potential gains and losses and the accrued actual losses and failures from the time of our conception onwards.

As a consequence, we start our life in the womb without any pressures as we are totally comfortable in our mother's womb, which is gradually changing as we are developing our own perception of reality.

In doing so, we are increasingly affected by the problems of the past, as some of the 'potential' losses may have become 'actual' losses that are now haunting us to the point where we just can't cope anymore.

The matter is compounded by our innate desire to find the limits of our comfort zone, as we can see in the behaviour of a two year old and the tantrums if it doesn't get what it wants, which can be a nightmare.

The phenomenon doesn't change much in principle as we grow up and continue to test our limits and the limits of others with respect to the satisfaction of our basic needs and our interaction needs.

The concept is of course representing the process of trial and error, whereby 'we' are bound to cause many problems which are hopefully solved by others, if not the businesses of industry and government.

The phenomenon of our comfort zone gives us an insight into the difference between the brain and the mind, whereby the brain does not have any responsibility relating to the process of trial and error.

By the same token, the brain is not responsible for creating the businesses of industry and government, whose sole purpose is to improve our quality of life until we have reached a status of 'mind over matter'.

The aspired status is synonymous with a minimal 'Cost of Living' and pursuit of the great unknown to the point where the human race cannot be advanced any further, in which lies the reality of a Paradise.

So how are we doing when it comes to the adequacy of the products and services (nutrient cycle or basic needs) and the fairness of the social controls (energy flow or interaction needs) of the modern world?

As it stands, we seem to be caught between a rock and a hard place as we are unable to go back (to the hunting and gathering), and our imagined expectations of the near and distant future cause us to procrastinate.

In order to get a better understanding of our current status as a cosmic fetus in the making, we have to refer to the evolution of our bodies and minds and the symptoms relating to 'The Elements of Good & Evil'.

In that context, the current status of our social progress is associated with the phenomenon of a Paradox insomuch that the democratic system is only designed to 'see to the needs of some of its stakeholders'.

The proof can be seen in the aspirations of the average business of industry and perception of reality relating to its purpose, which is frequently stated in the form of a 'Mission Statement', as illustrated below:

"The purpose of our company is to increase the intrinsic value of our common stock.

We are not in business to grow bigger for the sake of size, become more diversified, make the most or best of anything, provide jobs, have the most modern plants, the happiest customers, lead in new product development, or to achieve any other status which has no relation to the economic use of capital.

Any or all of these may be, from time to time, a means to our objective, but means and ends must never be confused.

We are in business solely to improve the inherent value of the ordinary shareholders' equity in the company".

Under the circumstances, the management system would only treat the symptoms relating to the other stakeholders until the 'inherent value of the ordinary <u>shareholder's</u> equity in the company' is affected.

Others have a different view as they claim that:

"We will deliver the highest value to our customers, suppliers, employees and shareholders as the premier technology, marketing, distribution and services company.

And again, others claim that: *"Profitability is not the purpose of, but limiting factor on, business enterprise, whereby profit is not the explanation, cause or rationale of business decisions, but a test of their validity.*

Profitability allows a business to sustain itself, but it would be dangerous to make profit the most important objective of a business.

A corporate culture that values profit above all else may lead to law breaking, excessive risk taking, unnecessary suffering for employees, or damage to society and the environment.

This takes us to the father of modern management, Dr. Peter Drucker, who believed that:

"*A business enterprise has two basic functions: marketing and innovation.*

If we want to know what a business is, we have to start with its purpose, which must lie outside the business itself, in fact, it must lie in society, since a business enterprise is an organ of society.

There is only one valid definition of business purpose: to create a customer who is the foundation of a business and keeps it in existence.

The customer alone gives employment, and it is to supply the customer that society entrusts wealth-producing resources to the business enterprise.

Because it is the purpose to create a customer, any business enterprise has two—and only two—basic functions: marketing and innovation.

And whilst Dr. Drucker encapsulates 'The Product Cycle' and the needs of the customer, he was nevertheless ignoring the needs and expectations of, and the support for the business from, the remaining stakeholders.

In doing so, 'The Elements of Good & Evil' may be awakened within the suppliers, the employees, possibly the shareholders and last but not least, the community at large, if not the entire human race.

The latter may be associated with the growing world wide consumerism and the ever-increasing competition between the developing nations and the developed nations, much of which is based on price.

Under the circumstances, the developed nations are inclined to focus on the development of new and exciting products and services, or value, whilst the developing nations are focusing on the affordability aspects.

At the same time, every product has a limited life span as the customers express their needs and expectations relating to 'Our Ultimate Purpose in Life', as illustrated below under "The Product Cycle of Life & Death".

The Product Cycle of Life & Death

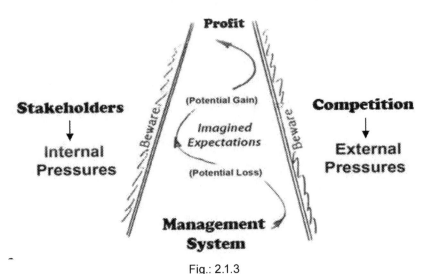

Fig.: 2.1.3

The illustration portrays the attitudes of the stakeholders and the associated internal pressures on the profitability of the business versus the nearest competitor and the associated external pressures.

In the case of the stakeholders and the community in particular, their case is frequently represented by a pressure group and a myriad of rules and regulations relating to their respective needs and wants.

The phenomenon is representing 'The Battle of Nature and Nurture' and the limits relating to the adequacy of our basic needs and the fairness of our interaction needs in our role as a customer and supplier, etc.

'The Battle of Nature & Nurture' took a new turn with the arrival of the Industrial Revolution and the transition to new manufacturing processes in the period from about 1760 to some time between 1820 and 1840.

This transition included going from hand production methods to machines, new chemical manufacturing and iron production processes, improved efficiency of water power, the increasing use of steam power and the development of machine tools.

It also included the change from wood and other bio-fuels to coal, which began in Great Britain and within a few decades had spread to Western Europe and the United States.

The Industrial Revolution marks a major turning point in history as almost every aspect of daily life was influenced in some way, as average income and population began to exhibit unprecedented sustained growth.

In the words of Nobel Prize winner Robert E. Lucas, Jr., "For the first time in history, the living standards of the masses of ordinary people have begun to undergo sustained growth, none of which was ever mentioned by the classical economists, not even as a theoretical possibility.

With the Industrial Revolution began an era of per-capita economic growth in capitalist economies and economic historians are in agreement that the onset of the Industrial Revolution is the most important event in the history of humanity since the domestication of animals and plants.

The First Industrial Revolution evolved into the Second Industrial Revolution in the transition years between 1840 and 1870, when technological and economic progress gained momentum with the increasing adoption of steam-powered boats, ships, railways, the large scale manufacture of machine tools and the increasing use of steam powered factories.

This brings us back to the current situation and the various interpretations of what a business is all about, as we are getting a mixed message relating to the business owners on one hand and the business advisers and schools on the other.

The problem would not apply to physicians and the central purpose of their profession, which is "To save lives", like the scientists is "To make new discoveries" and the educators "To teach the next generation."

But what would happen if we asked the same question of executives, entrepreneurs, managers, stockbrokers, consultants and the many others whose careers fall under the heading of "business"?

It is likely there would be no consensus among them about the purpose for their profession.

And whilst some might believe that their purpose is to maximize shareholder profit, others might cite a service to community whilst some others again might emphasize their personal goals and interests.

And so we are left to believe that, unlike other professionals, managers simply do not have the same overarching understanding of why they do what they do.

This is not the way it was at the onset of management education, when Joseph Wharton founded 'The Wharton School at the University of Pennsylvania' in Philadelphia in 1881.

That is, he believed that the school's guiding purpose was to graduate students who would *"serve the community skilfully as well as faithfully in offices of trust and to aid in maintaining sound financial morality."*

These days, the morality has somewhat eroded and, even though some schools still teach ethics, corporate social responsibility and self assessment, they have yet to adopt a universal sense of purpose.

This brings us back to Wallace B. Donham's address to the North-Western University about 'The History of Corporate Social Responsibility and Sustainability', the concern for which is as old as trade and business itself.

For example, commercial logging operations together with laws to protect forests can be traced back to almost 5,000 years.

Other laws can be traced back to Ancient Mesopotamia around 1700 BC, when King Hammurabi introduced a code in which builders, innkeepers or farmers were put to death if their negligence caused the deaths of, or major inconvenience to, local citizens.

In Ancient Rome senators grumbled about the failure of business to contribute sufficient taxes to fund their military campaigns, whilst in 1622 disgruntled shareholders in the Dutch East India Company started issuing pamphlets complaining about management secrecy and "self enrichment".

With industrialisation, the impacts of business on society and the environment assumed an entirely new dimension whereby the "corporate paternalists" of the late nineteenth and early twentieth centuries used some of their wealth to support philanthropic ventures.

By the 1920s discussions about the social responsibilities of business had evolved into what we can recognise as the beginnings of the modern 'Corporate Social Responsibility and Sustainability' movement.

At the same time, the businesses of industry and government have still not learned how to handle their corporate social responsibility, nor do they recognise the magnitude of their responsibilities for the future of civilisation.

That is, almost a century later our concerns are still the same as we face the concerns about the role of business in society, from internet "spam" to genetically modified foods, many of which are not very different to those being raised in the 1920s.

On that note, let us have a look at the role of business in society in the context of the human body and the various organs 'feeding' the body with goods and services, as illustrated below under "The Human Organization".

The Human Organization

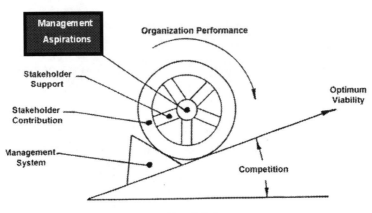

Fig.: 2.1.4

The illustration is portraying the 'Organization Performance' (or lack thereof) as a reflection of the Stakeholder Support for, and the Stakeholder Contribution to, the 'Optimum Viability' of the business.

In that context, the 'Stakeholder Support' is associated with the prevailing 'Human Resource Management' practices, whereas the 'Stakeholder Contribution' is associated with the 'Business Process Management'.

As to the 'Stakeholder Support' for the business, we are basically referring to its relationship with, and dependency on, the customer, supplier, employee, shareholder and the community at large, and vice verse.

Depending on the 'Management Aspirations', the business may:

(1) aim to lead the market through insight and foresight;
(2) wait until the nearest competitor is becoming a threat;
(3) be caught up in a cycle of continuous problem solving.

The dynamics of 'The Human Organization' are not unlike our body and the performance of the internal organs and cells in response to 'our' aspirations to realize a potential gain or prevent a potential loss.

And whilst the internal organs and cells are controlled by the 'SOUL' to the point where they may be pushed to the limits of their natural fitness for purpose, the same applies to the business and 'Our Ultimate Purpose'.

That is, providing the interaction needs of the stakeholders are administered fairly, in which case the stakeholders may want to contribute towards the business process until they reach the limits of their acquired fitness.

And whilst the stakeholders' energy and feelings are not accounted for on the balance sheet and/or financial bottom line of the business of industry, it does appear on "The Emotional Bottom Line", as illustrated below.

The Emotional Bottom Line

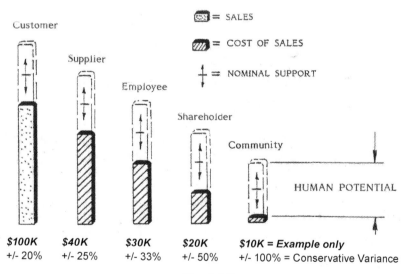

Fig.: 2.1.5

As it stands, the average business of industry is adopting the behaviour of a Paradox as it 'sees only to the needs of some of its stakeholders', where the focus is on predominantly on a potential win-win outcome.

In doing so, the best the remaining stakeholders can do is to give the business their 'nominal support' whilst adopting the behaviour of a Paradox themselves, which is bound to affect the performance of the business.

In that context, each stakeholder has an emotional relationship with the business which can be expressed in the form of a conservative variance of its 'Return on Investment', ranging from +/- 20% to +/- 100%.

For example, the average customer will happily pay 20% above the average price if the product is really exciting, novel, different and worth having, and the same applies to the negative dimension or attitude.

Likewise, the benefit of a reliable and trustworthy supplier of quality materials is costing at least 25% less than the average supplier who is not too concerned about the quality of its products and services.

We only have to look at the nuisance value of a raw material or a component that is fowling up the process, not to mention the damaged equipment and the reputation if the faulty product gets through to the customer.

This takes us to the employee who is known to use and abuse the system whenever he gets a chance, which does not apply to everybody, but it does happen, and we wouldn't want to put a price tag on it.

By the same token, the impact of this type of nuisance value on the rest of the team in terms of its cohesiveness, striving and general morale is not good either, not to mention the willful damage and stoppages.

But then again, we are not here to pass judgement as we are assuming a conservative +/-33% on the cost of employing human beings, without which we just couldn't run a business, as much as we might like to.

At the same time, the highly skilled, motivated and informed employee is bound to contribute at least twice as much to the bottom line than its negative counterpart, and there is a lot of evidence to back this up.

As to the shareholder, he/she is deemed to have a min. variance of +/- 50%, the reason for which lies in his/her interest in, and financial support for, the business culminating in its distinction in the market place.

And so we come to the 'conservative' +/- 100% variance relating to the cost of the community and the environment at large, for which the business may not be responsible, yet paying for in many ways.

We could start with the 'non-commercial opportunities' relating to the unemployed, the cost of crime, littering, vandalism, pollution, alcoholism, drugs, the poor and a myriad of other costs we can well do without.

If we were to quantify 'The Emotional Bottom Line' in $ terms for a given business, we could start by establishing the approximate 'potential gains' and 'actual losses' associated with the current business practice.

For the sake of the argument, we will 'assume' the average customer support for the business amounts to a $100K Sales versus a $40K + $30K + $20K + $10K = $100K Cost of Sales, as illustrated above.

In doing so, we may be surprised to find there is a huge difference between 'The Worst Case Scenario' and 'The Best Case Scenario' relating to the Sales and the Cost of Sales, respectively, whereby the:

Best Case Scenario = $120K Sales vs. $30 + $20 + $10 + $0 = $60K Cost of Sales.

Worst Case Scenario = $80K Sales vs. $50 + $40 + $30 + $20 = $140K C. of Sales.

The results are an astounding $120K Sales to a $60K Cost of Sales = $60K Potential Profit for the Best Case Scenario versus an $80K Sales to a $140K Cost of Sales = $60K Potential Loss for the Worst Case.

If we apply Dr. Peter Drucker's believes that *"A business enterprise has only two basic functions: marketing and innovation",* we might miss out on the potential gains and actual losses relating to the Cost of Sales.

On the other hand, the business may develop a power 'over' the customer in the form of a monopoly in the market which may allow it to charge whatever it likes as it predates on the customer in no uncertain terms.

By all accounts, there is many a business making a good profit in the guise of a Parasite or a Predator on the community, which may even be tolerated by the majority of people who may be similarly inclined.

Let us apply the above to our conscious awareness of the potential gains and losses relating to 'The Emotional Bottom Line' of the business, as illustrated below under "The Stakeholder Support".

The Stakeholder Support

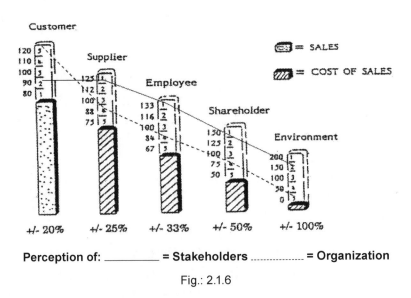

Perception of: _____ = Stakeholders .... = Organization

Fig.: 2.1.6

The picture says it all when it comes to 'The Management Opportunities', the realization of which begins with the communication gap between the Organization and its Stakeholders, one and all.

Note: The variance is based on the management strategy to:

1 = Ignore all Symptoms

2 = Address Major Symptoms

3 = Stop Problems from recurring

4 = Prevent Problems from occurring

5 = Facilitate Continuous Improvements

And so we proceed to inform the management of our findings, upon which the 'Management Aspirations' may be revealed in the form of its unofficial and unchanging pursuit of the status of a Parasite or a Predator.

On the other hand, the management may want to investigate the 'known & measurable' communication gap further in line with its responsibility for the sustainability of the business in the short and long term.

If so, our first course of action would be to identify the nature of the interaction, or 'communication gap', between the management and the employees, as illustrated below under "The Interaction Analysis".

The Interaction Analysis

TYPES	%	WISH	ACTUAL	POSITIVE 3	2	1	PERCEPTION 0	1	NEGATIVE 2	3
INSTRUCTED	10									
CONSULTED	15									
INCLUDED	20									
DELEGATED	45									
LEFT ALONE	10									

x = *management's perception of reality*   ⟶ *Communication* Gap ⟵

• = *employee's perception of reality*

Fig. 2.1.7

The illustration is portraying the 'Communication Gap' between leadership style and the inherent potential of the employees who were largely at stage 4 and only too willing to apply their fitness to a purpose.

That is, they wanted to be instructed when it came to the job in hand, consulted with respect to their level of fitness, included in the setting of targets and then delegated a responsibility relating to its achievement.

Instead, they were frustrated by the leadership style which was to control that urge with an array of instructions that did not necessarily reflect the acquired fitness level of the employees, one and all.

To make matters worse, the largest group of 45 is also the most frustrated group as they are only consulted with respect to their ability to perform a given task without being delegated any kind of meaningful responsibility.

When we talk to the individual groups, the first group of 10 is complaining about their situation, but not prepared to do anything about it, whereas the second group of 15 is condemning the leader.

The situation worsens as we get to the third group of 20, some of which are already looking for a job, whereas the fourth group is plotting the demise of the organization by considering their options in opposition.

As to the fifth and last group of 10, some of them are actually talking to the main shareholders in an attempt to take over the leadership with a plan of action that is designed to remedy the problem in hand.

This raises the question of the investors' or shareholders' perception of value for money or 'worthy of investing' in what may be perceived as an irresponsible act that is bound to affect the community at large.

That is, sooner or later the stakeholders will 'wise up' and/or 'rise up' against the business of industry and/or government, which are now clearly identified as a Parasite or Predator on the community at large.

On that note, let us look at the potential losses associated with "The Business Process" from the quote submission, order placement, process planning and process operation to the process review, as illustrated below.

The Business Process

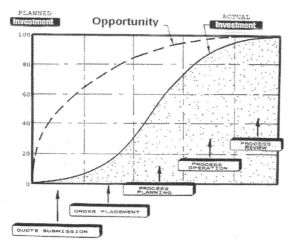

Fig.: 2.1.8

The illustration is portraying the 'The Business Process' and the 'Opportunity' for a 'Right the First Time' outcome, whereby most of the opportunity (60 % plus) may be allocated to the 'Quote Submission' stage.

Another 20% may be allocated to the 'Order Placement' stage, after which the opportunity is becoming increasing depleted until the actual versus planned investment can be measured at the 'Process Review' stage.

This brings us to 'The Perception of Reality' relating to the optimum viability of the business in the short and long terms, the short term of which is often associated with the 'Opportunity Curve' and the pursuit of sales.

Under the circumstances, the sales and marketing people may resort to a myriad of 'tricks of the trade' from the questionable connection of the product value with the female body, a famous person or other image to straight out lies.

The tendency has led to a number of pressure groups representing the customer above all, the main purpose of which was to create a level playing field for the importing and exporting of goods and services.

In that context, recognized bodies of knowledge or third parties have seen fit to create international standards for the manufacture and provision of a myriad of goods and services, as well as a Quality Assurance System.

The QA System was designed to cover the entire business process from the quote submission to the process review, where the ultimate intent of the system was to prevent potential problems from happening.

As a consequence, a buyer in country A may request that his supplier in country B provide a valid certificate of conformance issued by a government recognized third party, and vice versa, as in company B to company A.

Unfortunately, the conformance did not include 'The Stakeholder Support' for the certification and its ongoing compliance, which was audited on a periodical basis so as to ensure the continuity of the conformance.

Under the circumstances, many a so called compliance was nothing more than a scam, as some companies produced false information and records that were often accepted by an overworked or frustrated auditor.

Similar scenarios can be seen in the areas of 'OHS' or 'Occupational Health and Safety', Environmental Protection, Food Safety, Disability Services, Health Care in Hospitals and many, many more.

And so are reminded once again of Wallace B. Donham's prophetic claim that *"the world's problems would not be solved through governmental or police intervention, but from within on a higher ethical plane".*

If any, the Military style of intervention is only going to produce more criminals, as the employees and other stakeholders of the business have no choice but to go along with the charade, or lose their job.

We might be able to identify with the scenario where we walk into a medical centre and find a long line of people waiting to be served, and so we join the queue as we wait for our turn and have a look around.

In doing so, we notice a 'Mission Statement' on the wall making all sorts of heart warming claims about the 'Management Aspirations' and certification by a third party relating to the provision of quality services.

The item that catches our attention more so than the rest is about the desire to 'exceed the expectations of the customer', upon which we get up and address the queue with respect to their expectations at the time.

As it happened, nobody was happy or satisfied with the service, upon which we go to the counter and inform the receptionist of the discrepancy, only to find out that she was totally unaware of the statement.

At the same time, she hurriedly informs us that "I am only working here you know" and the fact that nobody else was complaining, so there, suggesting that 'we' might have a problem and not the management.

The experience reminds us of the story of the frogs in the pond and the gradual increase in the water temperature, which doesn't seem to bother the frogs as they gently slide into a situation of semi-consciousness.

And as they accept the situation without a complaint or desire to leave the pond, they are gradually approaching the inevitable, in which lies a moral that may well apply to the human race and the cosmic foetus.

As it stands, we are witnessing a 'stable & predictable' human condition that is based on lies, distortions of the truth, ignorance, apathy, favouritism, cronyism, opportunism and a myriad of other diseases of the mind.

And whilst we accept the fact that the world is on a downward slide, we are feeling helpless as we become the victims of our own misperceptions of reality, as illustrated below under "The Fool on the Hill".

The Fool on the Hill

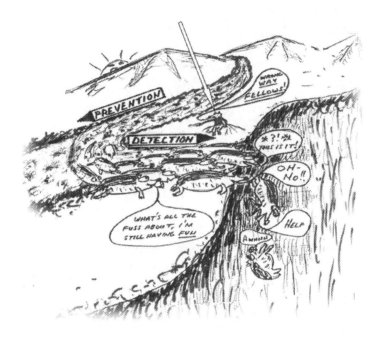

Fig.: 2.1.9

As to 'The Fool on the Hill', this can be related to the visionaries of this world like Socrates, who unfortunately was forced to drink poison for his 'Foolishness' according to the powers prevailing some 400 years BCE.

Many other advanced thinkers were either labelled as crazy or put to death like:

Christopher Columbus who believed that the earth was round and bitterly attacked for it.

Giordano Bruno who claimed that the earth was not the centre of the universe, for which he was burned at the stakes.

The Wright brothers who were ridiculed for believing a machine could fly.

Andreas Vesalius who is known as the father of anatomy and was originally labelled an imposter and heretic for his discoveries.

William Harvey who was disgraced as a physician for believing that blood was pumped by the heart and travelled through arteries.

Galileo Galilei who taught that the earth rotates around the sun and thrown in prison for it.

More recently, people like Wallace B. Donham, Harvard Business School's second dean, and many others have been treated with more tolerance and freedom of speech, whilst they were largely ignored, nevertheless.

This brings us back to the long term viability of the business and the emerging pressure groups, some of which come under the heading of 'Ethical Consumerism' that is based on the concept of 'dollar voting'.

The term "ethical consumer" was first popularised by the UK magazine the Ethical Consumer which was first published in 1989 with a 'ratings table' inspired by the ethical investment movement.

The ratings tables awarded companies negative marks (and from 2005 overall scores) across a range of ethical and environmental categories such as 'animal rights', 'human rights' and 'pollution and toxics'.

Such ethical and environmental ratings have subsequently become commonplace both in providing criteria based consumer information and business-to-business corporate responsibility and sustainability ratings.

Similar pressures groups are emerging on the criteria based consumer information on the rights of the supplier, the employee and the shareholders, all of which is adding up to the emerging powers of 'Morality'.

This raises the question of "How can the management ensure the optimization of the emotional bottom line and the sustainability of the business without having to resort to the process of trial and error?"

The answer lies in the management aspirations reflecting the ultimate purpose of the business on one hand, and the needs and expectations of the stakeholders on the other, as illustrated under "MAPS for the Future".

MAPS for the Future

"The purpose of our business is to create products and services for which there is a demand in the chosen market, the continuity of which is based on our commitment to marketing and innovation.

In order to do so, the business needs the support of its stakeholders if it is to survive in the short and long term, whereby the future depends on its 'Mutual Appreciation and Performance Standards'.

'Mutual Appreciation' equates to the needs of the stakeholders being catered for by the business, and vice versa, where the 'Performance Standards' reflect the minimum expectations of either party.

The resulting 'Team Spirit' and 'Team Effort' are deemed to produce an ever increasing 'Quality of Life' for the customer, supplier, employee, shareholder and the community as the stakeholders of a thriving business."

Fig.: 2.1.10

The concept is not dissimilar to our aspirations as a thinking mind relating to the creation of a cosmic foetus, the continuity of which is essentially based 'our' commitment to the pursuit of the great unknown.

In order to do so, the individual needs the ongoing support of the organs and cells if it is to survive in the short and long term, whereby its future depends on the 'Mutual Appreciation and Performance Standards'.

In that context, the human body is working to a system of two-way communication that is deemed ultimately fair, whereas the businesses of industry are still in the process of developing such a system.

The biggest problem facing society these days with the development of such a system is associated with the widening gap between the rich and the poor, whereby the rich think that 'they' have the most to lose.

At the same time, most of their problems come from the widening gap, as we can see in the problems of the modern world, where the power 'over' the people is no longer valid when it comes to the element of fairness.

On that note, how happy are the rich and famous when it comes to the satisfaction of their basic needs and their interaction needs these days?

For all we know, money doesn't make us happy according to the social media, yet many of us are still dreaming about winning the lottery or becoming a millionaire, the aftermath of which can be disastrous.

At the same time, there are many rich people out there who know how to handle their money and wealth, but they seem to be in the minority, nevertheless, as they focus on the needs of others as well as their own.

When we look at the history of the human race, it seems almost inconceivable that we will ever reach a point of:

A *'Team Spirit'* and *'Team Effort'* that is deemed to produce an ever increasing *'Quality of Life'* for the customer, supplier, employee, shareholder and the community as the stakeholders of a thriving business."

At the same time, we have no alternative unless we are prepared to give up our long term sustainability in favour of a short gain, be it at the expense of others, like the stakeholders which we dependent upon.

Be it as it may, in the long term our personal happiness and sustainability as a human race is basically associated with the minimum needs and expectations of the business and the stakeholders alike.

And from here on, there is nothing stopping us from adding to the expectations as we focus on the potential gains with a sense of 'Team Spirit' and 'Team Effort' that is bound to benefit the business and stakeholders, alike.

In that context, the concept of the 'Ethical Consumerism' will eventually cover the entire spectrum of stakeholders which, in turn, is going to shape the social conscience of the community and its social controls.

And as the 'Ethical Consumerism' is becoming increasingly 'stable & predictable' the world over, the forces of Nature will gradually adapt us to 'The Higher Ethical Plane' until we reach a state of mind over matter.

In the meantime, the individual, the products and services and social controls are going through a cycle of life and death, as discussed under 'The Ritual of Life & Death', 'The Ritual of Industry' and 'The Ritual of Government'.

As to the latter, 'The Higher Ethical Plane' is slowly going to encompass the entire human race in line with our growing conscious awareness of 'Our Ultimate Purpose in Life' and the creation of a cosmic fetus.

This takes us to "The Power Cycle of Life & Death" and the next level of a Panacea or cure-all that is going to drive the human race one step closer to its ultimate existence here on earth, as illustrated below.

The Power Cycle of Life & Death

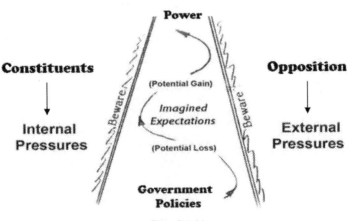

Fig.: 2.1.11

The illustration is reflecting 'The Evolution of Power' and the perceived fairness of the prevailing social controls as per the constituents or residents of a district and the opposing political parties and their views.

A typical set of policies may entail economic policy, environment and resources policy, law and justice policy and social policy, each of which is further supported by rules and regulations.

Economic Policy refers to the actions that governments take in the economic field which covers the systems for setting interest rates and government budget as well as the labour market, national ownership, and many other areas of government interventions into the economy.

Such policies are often influenced by international institutions like the International Monetary Fund or World Bank as well as political beliefs and the consequent policies of parties.

Environment and Resources Policy is primarily about a sustainable environment.

Law and Justice Policy refers to the demands for a criminal justice system, especially in relation to the prevention of violence and property crime through stricter criminal penalties.

Whilst supporters of "law and order" argue that effective deterrence combined with incarceration is the most effective means of crime prevention, opponents of law and order argue that a system of harsh criminal punishment is ultimately ineffective because it does not address the underlying or systemic causes of crime.

"Law and order" is a recurring theme in political campaigns around the world, where candidates may exaggerate or even manufacture a problem with law and order, or characterise their opponents as "weak" on the issue, to generate public support.

The expression also sometimes carries the implication of arbitrary or unnecessary law enforcement, or excessive use of police powers.

Social Policy primarily refers to guidelines, principles, legislation and activities that affect the living conditions conducive to human welfare.

It seeks to understand the theory and evidence drawn from a wide range of social science disciplines, including economics, sociology, psychology, geography, history, law, philosophy and political science.

Social Policy is focused on those aspects of the economy, society and policy that are necessary to human existence and the means by which they can be provided.

These basic human needs include: food and shelter, a sustainable and safe environment, the promotion of health and treatment of the sick, the care and support of those unable to live a fully independent life; and the education and training of individuals to a level that enables them fully to participate in their society".

Social policy often deals with wicked problems.

As it stands, the policies represent a nightmare of do's and don'ts that require an army of people focusing on the trials and errors of our forefathers without due consideration of our growing mental capacity.

Given the political awareness of, and response to, 'Our Ultimate Purpose in Life' is virtually non-existent; we are not surprised by the prevailing powers over the people, which can really get up our collective noses.

And whilst the emphasis is on the detection of our failure to comply with the myriad of rules and regulations, they are designed to take the dignity out of our life, as everyone is presumed guilty until proven otherwise.

At the same time, the 'guilty' are likely to become social outcast as the system addresses the symptoms of an outdated model of social control that will only increase the frequency and severity of the symptoms.

Under the circumstances, the constituents may combine their resources in the form of a political pressure group or two, the reality of which can be seen in 'The Political Spectrum' and the left and right wing policies.

The right and left-wing spectrum originally referred to the seating arrangements in the French parliament after the Revolution, where communism and tyranny are usually regarded as being on the left, and anarchy and liberty on the right.

Liberalism can mean different things in different contexts, sometimes on the left (social liberalism), sometimes on the right, (economic liberalism) whilst politics that reject the conventional left-right spectrum is known as (idio)syncretic politics, and those with an intermediate outlook are classified as centrists or moderates.

By all accounts, 'The Political Spectrum' represents a nightmare of political chicanery consisting of clever, dishonest talk or behaviour that is used to deceive people with respect to the needs of the community.

This takes us to 'The New World Order' and The Commission on Global Governance, an independent group of 28 public figures who were inspired by the belief that the end of the cold war offered opportunities to build a more co-operative, safer and fairer world.

It presents proposals for improving the world's governance and better managing its affairs in a report named Our Global Neighbourhood which was published in 1995—the year the United Nations marked its fiftieth anniversary.

The message of the report was encapsulated in its title and the book-length report was commended by such world figures as Nelson Mandela, Gro

Harlem Brundtland and Vaclav Havel, which led to worldwide interest and appearance in 15 languages.

The Commission's two Co-Chairmen were Ingvar Carlsson, former Prime Minister of Sweden, and Shridath (Sonny) Ramphal, former Secretary-General of the Commonwealth, from Guyana, whilst its members were drawn from all continents.

In 1999, the Commission issued a further report as the United Nations prepared to hold a Millennium Assembly and Summit in 2000 and address two subjects: involving civil society and improving world economic management.

Reforming the United Nations

The Commission's recommendations centre principally on the United Nations, the only forum in which governments come together regularly to tackle world problems, where 'Our Global Neighbourhood' suggests how the UN should be revitalised so it can better respond to the needs of the modern world—a world that has changed in many ways since the UN was formed in 1945.

The report includes proposals to:

Reform the Security Council, so that it becomes more representative and maintains its legitimacy and credibility

Set up an Economic Security Council to have more effective—and more democratic—oversight of the world economy

Establish a United Nations Volunteer Force so that the Security Council can act more quickly in emergencies

Vest the custody of the global commons in the Trusteeship Council, which has completed its original work

Treat the security of people and of the planet as being as important as the security of states

Strengthen the rule of law worldwide

Give civil society a greater voice in governance.

Explore ways to raise new funds for global purposes, e.g. a tax on foreign currency movements, and charges for using flight lanes, sea-lanes and other common global resources.

The Commission calls for a global neighbourhood ethic and commitment to core global values that can command respect across frontiers of race and religion. It also makes a plea for enlightened leadership that looks beyond the next election.

The report makes clear that in urging action to improve governance, the Commission is not advocating movement towards world government.

A commentator who considered several reports that addressed issues of international reform had this to say:

"Of the dozen studies reviewed here, arguably the most influential and widely read happens to be the most ambitious: the 1995 report, Our Global Neighbourhood, by the Commission on Global Governance . . . . The implementation track record of its proposal has been mixed.

Yet Our Global Neighbourhood had a powerful message, one that pulled its seemingly disparate parts together and that still animates much of the internationalist literature.

It was neither the first nor the last report to stress the need to find better ways of handling transnational problems, but it did an unusually effective job of conceptualising the practice and challenges of global governance . . . ."

Once the proposals for improving the world's governance are ratified by individual nations, they become INTERNATIONAL LAW, which may include a world court, a global tax, and a global police force.

The coming one world government is being set up in the political arena under the flag of the United Nations, through organizations such as the Trilateral Commission, Council of Foreign Relations, the Royal Institute of International Affairs, the Bilderbergers, and the Club of Rome whose members include many world leaders, media personalities and other influential people.

The published goal of the Council of Foreign Relations for example is a one world government, and although most have never heard of many of these groups, they do exist, and they are very influential.

Whilst the core of these groups holds to "illuminist" philosophy, a second focus is on economics with free trade agreements, the International Monetary Fund, World Bank and the Bank of International Settlements.

The coming global monetary crisis is intended to institute a universal debt-based currency controlled by the International Financiers and issued to individuals against biometric identification cards. (This is all about control!)

The third area of focus is religion, where organizations like the World Council of Churches and the Parliament of World Religions were established to introduce a new world religion based on a religious/humanist philosophy.

Careful attention should be paid when we study the documents and reports published by the United Nations and related organizations, the philosophy of which is now being taught in the education system and has been implemented under programs such as Goals 2000.

The general perception is that the New World Order will be SOCIALISM, whereby the individual will be subservient to the state and rights and power reside in, and derive from, the state, not the individual.

United Nations documents all speak of collectivism as they claim that private ownership and management of property is not to the benefit of the human race, as these things are cloaked in a pleasant language, and most people are taken in and deceived.

From a sceptic's perspective, the New World Order we will be in serfdom to the controlling elite! We will have no liberty, and no rights, whilst the State will look after us for our best interests, which is exactly what socialism is.

The government becomes involved in every aspect of personal life as today we require a license for so many things like in Australia, farmers now require permission to farm the land they own—This is not freedom.

In the New World Order, private ownership of property will be abolished and we will only own what we need "after all this is best for the world," and so "We need to be looked after."

Terms such as 'sustainable development' could well mean a state of depopulation and serfdom, as the masses continue to fall for lie after lie and studies in history will confirm that there have been very few free societies.

Those that were free were either overthrown or fell into the trap of socialism, totally unaware of the dangers until it was too late, like Socialism (communism) which has always been implemented through deception.

History portrays a repetitive phenomenon . . . enslavement-revolt-freedom-apathy-enslavement, frequently followed revolution because the people did not realize that socialism was slavery, not freedom.

Today environment is being used to make people feel guilty, enticing them to accept socialism as necessary, while the environmental movement has been co-opted to strip private ownership of control and exploitation of resources.

Many environmental 'facts' are lies, exaggerations and unscientific claims to manipulate the masses in the classic Hegelian Dialectic: create the problem, create opposition to the problem, and then present your own predetermined solution.

So what do we make of 'The New World Order' and The Commission on Global Governance and the 'Conspiracy Theory' that we are going to be 'enslaved' by the international push to the left, as in Socialism?

The answer lies in our perception of reality relating to the element of fairness and 'The Survival of the Fairest' systems of social control or government of the world, as illustrated below under "The New World Order".

The New World Order

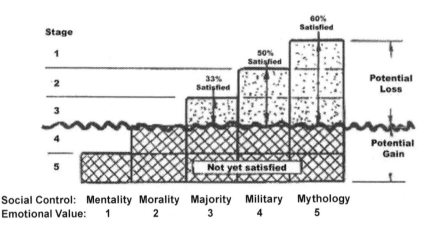

Fig.: 2.1.12

The illustration portrays 'The Battle of Nature & Nurture' and 'The Survival of the Fairest', whereby the power of Mythology represents our acquisition of a fitness for a higher purpose than 'The Survival of the Fittest'.

The battle can be seen in the instructions relating to what might be considered as 'animal behaviour' like sex in public, nudity, killing, rape, infidelity, marriage between siblings, food consumption and many more.

As it stands, the power 'over' the people has somewhat waned as we can see in the potential problems associated with the belief systems becoming actual problems that are threatening to destroy the world.

To a lesser extent, the power of the Military has lost its power 'over' the people as we can see in the potential problems associated with a dictator having become actual problems that are beyond our comprehension.

And to a lesser extent again, the power of the Majority is starting to lose its shine as the potential problems are becoming actual problems that are simply too difficult and complex for the elected party to solve.

At the same time, all of these power bases have their valid place within the context of society, as they represent the stepping stones for the next stage in our growth and development as a human race.

This takes us to the difficult aspect of their 'Need to Change' and the 'Potential Gains' derived from:

1. The powers of Mythology and their desire for a 'World Religion' comprising all belief and non-belief systems as well as the in-betweeners, the concept of which lies in the proposition of a 'Grand Order of Design' or 'GOD'.
2. The powers of the Military (or Police) and their desire for a system of positive motivation relating to the pursuit of the great unknown so as to advance the human race, which cannot be achieved through prohibition alone.
3. The powers of the Majority or democratic system of social control and their desire to represent the needs and expectations of 'all' the stakeholders without the reliance on a charismatic leader or similar figurehead.

Under the circumstances, it is not enough for one or two of the powers to 'See the Light', but rather the entire spectrum of powers, in which lies the key to 'The New World Order' and the salvation of the human race.

Given the social conscience is a reflection of our growing metal capacity and desire to be instructed, consulted, included, delegate or left alone in the context of government, 'we' are the key to 'The New World Order'.

In that context, the illustration is reflecting the current status of the world, where the powers of Mythology or belief systems are two thirds depleted, which is really shaking the foundation of their influence around the world.

And whilst the powers of Mythology may do their utmost to overcome these problems by referring to the 'Evil' associated with 'Our Ultimate Purpose in Life', this is not going to change their diminishing powers.

This takes us to the powers of the Military which are 50% depleted, and so they are equally balanced when it comes to their powers for dealing with the actual problems associated with that type of social control.

As a consequence, the powers of the Military (or police) may still be effective when it comes to one half of the population, whereas the other half of the population is likely to reject this type of unilateral social control

As it stands, the powers of the Military are not what they used to be in the good old days when you could steal from, enslave, or otherwise exploit the weak or change a person's mind with a threat or a weapon.

This takes us to the powers of the Majority which are 33% depleted, in which case the actual problems with this kind of social control are associated with the minority groups as well as the rich and powerful.

As to the first, the minority groups may resort to their becoming a financial burden or nuisance value to the community, which in turn is going to add to the cost of living whilst diminishing the quality of life.

Coming to the rich and powerful, they may be dreaming up a New World Order that is ultimately based on the power of Money, the Military and Mythology, in which lies a Pseudoscience of world proportion.

If so, what are their chances of success?

The answer lies once again with W. D Donham, according to which *"the world's problems would not be solved through governmental or police intervention, but from within on a higher ethical plane"*, or power of Morality.

On that note, let us summarise the personal cycle of life & death, the product cycle of life & death and the power cycle of life and death in the light of 'The Battle of Nature & Nurture' and 'Our Ultimate Purpose in Life'.

In that context, we have to accept the proposition of a cosmic foetus and the energy flow between the unconscious, the subconscious, the conscious mind, the super-conscious and the social conscience.

Secondly, we have to accept the fact that our genes are the ultimate 'barometer' when it comes to 'Our Ultimate Purpose in Life', the proof of which can be seen in the diseases of the body and the mind.

In doing so, the diseases are telling us that we have strayed off 'The Straight and Narrow' or out of our 'Comfort Zone' for too long, too often, by too much and/or by too many, and so it's back to the drawing board.

And whilst this may be one hell of a way to live our lives, run a business, a community, a nation and ultimately a united world that is sustainable beyond the planet earth, this is the only way it can be done.

Any other way like a 'Right the First Time' accomplishment of a goal would eliminate the pursuit of the great unknown, in which case 'The Process of Trial & Error' would not be required, and nor would we.

2.2   The Process of Trial & Error

And so we not only accept "The Process of Trial & Error" as an integral part of life here on earth and in the universe, but furthermore appreciate it for what it is—the reason for our existence, as illustrated below.

The Process of Trial & Error

Stage	Typical Management Strategy	Reference
1	Ignore the symptoms until a loss occurs	
2	Treat the symptom only until losses recur	*(Need to Change)*
3	Modify root causes to stop recurring losses	
4	Monitor critical causes so loss will not occur	*(Want to Compete)*
5	Improve the causes to optimize potential gains	

Fig.: 2.2.1

Note: According to the definition shown in the Wikipedia, '*Trial and Error* is a fundamental method of solving problems that is characterised by repeated, varied attempts which are continued until success, or until the agent stops trying.*'

If we apply the process to the business, the management is inclined to ignore the symptoms at first until the loss is starting to affect the bottom line, upon which it may treat the symptom only until the loss recurs.

If the known losses are threatening the survival of the business in the short term, the management may modify the root causes so as to prevent the same or similar problems from recurring time and again.

And so the business is slowly progressing from one stage to another until it is ready to compete against its nearest opposition or competitor, upon which the critical causes to its success are monitored.

In the process, the needs of 'all' the stakeholders will eventually be deemed as the critical causes to its sustainability and not just the customer, and so the business will take on the role of a Panacea or 'Cure All'.

Having been there and done that to the point where the sustainability of the business is pretty well assured in the near future, the business can devote itself to the ongoing improvement of the causes.

And the same principle applies to the businesses of government, and they will continue to drive us to the pinnacle of our existence until our basic needs and our interaction needs are 100% adequate and fair, forever.

So how are the businesses of industry and government around the world progressing with respect to 'The Process of Trial & Error' and the modification of the root causes relating to the world's biggest problems?

'The World's Biggest Problems' portal (web site) has a simple, clear mission: educating people all around the world about the biggest problems facing humanity.

These problems have two criteria; 1. They must be global in scope and 2. They must have the potential to rapidly escalate into a severe crisis, which takes us to:

a) Economic Collapse: Fragilities in the current global economy could tip the developed world into conditions not seen since the 1920s.

b) Peak Oil: Petroleum has powered the modern world for almost 100 years; today, many industry insiders say that we may be reaching a permanent peak in oil production.

c) Global Water Crisis: Over the last 50 years the human population has nearly tripled, while industrial pollution, unsustainable agriculture, and poor civic planning have decreased the overall water supply.

d) Species Extinction: Certain species that human beings depend upon for our food supply are going extinct; if their numbers fall too low we may face extinction ourselves.

e) Rapid Climate Change: While the debate rages on about the causes of climate change, global warming is an empirical fact. The problem is both a curse and blessing, in that people from different cultures will either have to work together or face mutual destruction.

If we go back to the 'simple and clear mission of educating people', let us assume we have educated everyone with respect to the world's greatest problems—and then what?

Does the simple fact of our global conscious awareness and sense of priority relating to the world's biggest problems give us the means or wherewithal to change the parasitical tendencies of the belief systems?

Likewise, does our global awareness give us the means to change the brutalities, genocides, mass killings, famines and a myriad of other socio-economic and socio-political problems associated with the military systems?

As it stands, we are not only made aware of the symptoms on a daily basis by the social media, but we also seem to have developed a kind of moral apathy or indifference relating to the biggest problems of the world.

What is reason behind our indifference and how can we overcome this barrier when it comes to the world's biggest problems?

One person who is looking for the answer is the Prime Minister of the United Kingdom, David Cameron, who is offering £1 million to anyone who can solve the world's biggest problem—whatever that might be.

Cameron studied Philosophy, Politics and Economics at Oxford and gaining a first class honours degree before he joined the Conservative Research Department and became Special Adviser to Norman Lamont, and then to Michael Howard.

He was Director of Corporate Affairs at Carlton Communications for seven years and is now asking people to determine the greatest challenge facing humanity today, such as finding a replacement for oil, producing low-cost food or eradicating malaria.

Once the trickiest issue has been decided, the Prime Minister will give away £1 million in cash to the person who successfully works out the answer.

The competition is modelled on the Longitude Prize launched by Parliament in 1714, which offered £20,000 to anyone who could discover how far east or west ships had sailed.

Sailors could work out their location north and south, and were able to determine their local time from the sun, however, they needed to know the time at a reference point in order to find out how far they had travelled east or west.

Many people thought the issue was impossible to solve, but the prize was eventually won by John Harrison, a working-class joiner as he designed a clock that that kept accurate time at sea and enabled sailors to work out their location.

Almost exactly 300 years on, Mr Cameron will set up a new Longitude Committee to gather suggestions and draw up a shortlist of problems facing the world, upon will the government will launch a race to solve the most difficult predicament

Sources said the prize may not actually be awarded for many years, as scientists in universities and companies have been wrestling with many of the world's most difficult problems for a long time.

A Downing Street source said: "We want people to think big like: What does the world need most and how can we achieve that? We are looking for the next penicillin, aeroplane or World Wide Web.

Can we grow limbs or create universal low carbon travel or do something that is really going to revolutionise what we do and how we live our lives— sending us sprinting ahead in the global race.

Note: We can see the emphasis on the 'how' of life on earth and the total absence of the 'why' of life, which is typical when it comes to our perception of reality relating to 'The Biggest Problems of the World'.

In doing so, the views of the government are nevertheless based on 'our' sense of priorities relating to the satisfaction of our basic needs and the potential problems having become actual problems of the world.

Speaking at a conference on science ahead of the G8 summit, Mr Cameron will say it is essential to "nurture new ideas" and "bend over backwards to attract the best and the brightest" to Britain.

Mr. Cameron is hosting the G8 summit of world leaders in Northern Ireland in 2013, pledging to promote an "ambitious practical and pro-business agenda that benefits everyone".

Another person who is looking for the answer is Christian Sarkar, a 'Guardian Sustainable Business Professional' as he poses the question "Can business solve the world's biggest problems by disruptive change?"

For example, market disruption propels change, but few companies venture into the largest untapped sector: the poor and, in our current state of economic distress, the last thing you'd expect is for business to start solving problems for people who are not their customers.

And yet, this is what Harvard business guru, Clayton Christensen, has been talking about since the mid-90s, as he points out that there are two ways to disrupt markets:

1. Low-end disruption occurs when a product or service starts as a simple application at the bottom of a market and then moves up market, eventually disrupting the leading competitors.

2. New market disruption occurs when business has not paid enough attention to a new or emerging market segment that is not being served by existing businesses in the industry.

In that context: What bigger market is there than the poor, and why are they not being served?

A not-so recent estimate puts the size of the market at $5trillion with 4 billion potential customers, but the reasons why the poor are not viewed as customers is not so clear.

According to the research, the top reasons businesses cite for not serving those at the base of the pyramid are as follows:

- Business model adjustments
- Business environment
- Operational partnerships
- Market or supplier development
- Funding partnerships

At the same time he states that according to him, there is another reason: The mindset of the company leadership, as too often senior executives focus on their most profitable customers, and ignore emerging markets because they are simply not viewed as big enough, or profitable enough, to make a difference. I

Instead, they focus on 10% of the market because it is profitable, ignoring the other 90% which is assumed to be unreachable or unservable, as one would expect from the Paradox business model.

When will companies start designing products and services for the other 90%?

There's a growing movement lead by entrepreneurs such as Paul Polak who don't view the poor as a social responsibility or charity.

Instead, the needs of the poor are viewed as a business opportunity as he points to the solar pumping systems that have been available for years, yet haven't been adopted at scale for one simple reason: they cost too much.

The purchase price of solar PV systems is too high to be competitive with diesel pumps, even though the fuel and repair costs of diesel pumps are astronomical.

By cutting the cost of solar pumping systems by 80%, Polak's Sunwater project is seeking to boost small farmer incomes, create tens of thousands of new jobs, and significantly lower carbon emissions.

He calls his design approach zero-based design, an approach that starts from scratch, making no assumptions about the technology and strategy that can best be used or created to address a specific problem.

A few innovators engage the poor not just as consumers, but as producers, distributors, and retailers in their business models and value chains.

Project Nurture is a $11.5m dollar partnership among The Coca-Cola Company, the Bill & Melinda Gates Foundation, and the international non-profit organisation, TechnoServe who are working together to build and strengthen the local ecosystem of mango and passion fruit producers and processors.

The goal is to double the fruit incomes of more than 50,000 smallholder farmers in Kenya and Uganda. Over the span of the project, all the players will develop the capabilities and commercial incentives to continue doing business together even after the project ends.

There is a growing understanding among policymakers that innovations in technology offer disruptive and transformative opportunities in the field of human rights, from the role of the internet in the Arab Spring, to the drama of WikiLeaks, technology and access to information have raised political stakes like never before.

Ushahidi, which means "testimony" in Swahili, was a website that was initially developed to map reports of violence in Kenya after the post-election fallout at the beginning of 2008.

Since then, it has grown into an anti-corruption and transparency mapping engine for anyone, anytime, anywhere, but it is still about the people and "How to fight corruption with online tools", says Tarik Nesh Nash.

Technology can empower citizens, raise awareness and pressure authorities, yet, technology cannot fight corruption; it cannot change cultures, detect problems, propose solutions or amend laws.

People can, and as we are building online tools, we should remember their reason for existence, that is, they should be part of a broader strategy of engagement and participation.

The idea that technology will solve everything is of course a false hope, despite the enthusiasm of the individual behind the new technologies across the world, since:

"The responsibility and burden for change lies with individuals and businesses that want to make a difference".

There used to be a popular story that private enterprise could do something that governments weren't very good at: create jobs. Is that still true?

According to Clayton Christensen, the current focus across on efficiency and cost-cutting is succeeding in destroying jobs for many and creating capital for few: "Disruptive innovations create jobs, whereas efficiency innovations destroy them."

Christensen has suggested that we change the capital gains tax rate so that it decreases the longer an investment is held, which would encourage investment for the long run and encourage real innovation, as opposed to short-term measures designed to boost the next quarter's results.

How will this change the world's biggest problem according to Real Clear Science's Alex Berezow who claims that the single biggest threat facing humanity is poverty, which is a mundane topic as it is neither sexy nor trendy, but it is nonetheless true?

His reasoning is based on the lack of adequate healthcare in the world's poorest countries and six of the ten leading causes of death by infectious diseases: lower respiratory infections, diarrhoea, AIDS, malaria, tuberculosis and neonatal infections.

In fact, microbiologists in particular would disagree that climate change is the world's #1 threat as their biggest fear is the terrifying rise of multi-drug resistant bacteria, as well as the ever-present threat of deadly viruses going pandemic, such as influenza and MERS . . . .

Did you know that 250,000 to 500,000 children go blind annually from vitamin A deficiency, half of whom die within 12 months?—You won't find that sad statistic on the front page (or on any page, for that matter) of our newspapers. But think about it. Comprehend it. It might just change your perspective on global priorities.

Berezow doesn't say climate change—and possibly catastrophic effects of weather, agriculture, and more—isn't cause for concern, but he rightly points out that climate change (formerly global warming) is a relatively slow-moving situation and one that we can adapt to in all sorts of ways.

But poverty and its effects—which are remediable through such easy interventions as cheap or free multivitamins and the creation of more potable water supplies—are with us right now. "Tackling the world's real problems," he notes, "doesn't make for exciting television." But it might actually make for a better world right now.

This takes us to the role of the church and 'Why' the Church exists as per The Ministry of the Saints and author: Ray V Stedman who wrote:

We will recognize instantly that this whole matter of the place of the church in the world today is a very confused issue as we are being told on one hand that;

The job of the church is to forget doctrinal preaching and desire for individual salvation and involve itself in the problems of human suffering and injustice.

The church, they say, belongs in the vanguard of the struggle for social justice and the reason Christianity is shunned by the world is because Christians will not dirty their hands or risk their reputations.

We are being told that Christians can only show their faith as Christians if they are willing to carry a placard in Alabama, risk jail in some picket line, join the fight for land reform, or the abolition of laws against homosexuality and adultery.

We are told that the church should be speaking to all the issues of life today and should be concerned about problems of metropolitan government, mass transportation, suburban segregation, equal representation in legislatures, and other problems that confront our modern world.

On the other side there is an equally vocal group which says the job of the church is to thunder against evil from the pulpit, to denounce Communism, and anti-Americanism, and, thus preserve, if possible, the blessings of bourgeois materialism for Christians to enjoy to the full.

They say we must attack with scorching language anyone who dares to raise questions about the Bible, or threaten the special privileges of Christians in modern society, where the theme of this group seems to be, "Come weal or come woe, the status is quo."

Now this polarity of view as to what the church should be, and how it should work, is a perfect example of the ability of the devil to drive people to extremes and thus weaken the faith of many and cast a cloud of obscurity over the truth.

Whilst the information is giving us an insight into Why the Church exists as per The Ministry of the Saints, the Catholic Church is trying to deal with its own problem, as we can see in the 5 challenges Pope Francis will face as the new leader of the Roman Catholic Church:

Governance

The function—some would say dysfunction—of the Roman Catholic Church's central administration is one of the profound issues facing the new pope. The Curia is still a mainly Italian affair, composed of officials who are supposed to support and implement the pope's vision, whilst many men dedicate their lives to this work.

But there are many even within the church who believe the Curia is in dire need of reform, as Cardinal John Olorunfemi Onaiyekan of Nigeria said recently to the Catholic News Service, "Jesus put the church in the hands of erring humans."

The "Vatileaks" scandal, the handling of the catastrophic sexual abuse cases around the world, questions over corruption in the Institute for Works of Religion (the Vatican Bank) and rumours and reports of ego-driven infighting have brought the Curia under intense criticism.

Geo-politics

The Catholic Church has lost a lot of its global punch, as in the years of John Paul II, the Vatican was a major player and the pope could use the phone and presidents answered and a speech by the pope could put issues of social and economic justice on the global stage.

But Benedict was a very different kind of pope—much less the global superstar, much more the theologian which led to the church losing much of its lustre on the world stage and his responsibility for this will be long debated by historians.

Relevancy

Whilst individual Catholics couldn't vote in the College of Cardinals, they can vote on the church with their feet, and their hearts, in which case there are 1.2 billion Catholics around the globe, but many have fallen away from the faith.

They don't go to church, baptize their babies, get married or seek much moral guidance from the church, some of which has to do with the seemingly endless string of sexual scandals around the globe, the remoteness and opaqueness of the Vatican hierarchy, the contested role of women, issues of sexuality and morality or just a lack of relevancy in everyday life.

The exodus of Catholics from the faith has the church spooked.

Practical problems

Given the size of the church, there is no end to the litany of regional challenges it faces: social and economic injustice, doctrinal issues and many very practical issues.

Francis must deal with the Vatican's financial affairs. A debate over the (non)-transparency—how money comes into and goes out of the church's financial institutions—caused the Italian central bank to shut down the Vatican's credit and debit transactions earlier this year.

The Vatican downplayed the incident and a European financial watchdog said the church had made progress, but needed to do more.

Work in progress

The Catholic Church is a work in progress and has been so for more than 2,000 years. In the 1960s, the Vatican II councils jettisoned the Latin mass and opened up a conversation.

Many say that conversation has stalled and are looking to Pope Francis to restart it, where the argument is that the church is facing its greatest challenges as its history is full of crises.

But Pope Francis is confronted with problems under the scrutiny and demands of a globalized media and the unforgiving and instantaneous presence of the internet—a platform where scandals, missteps, secrets and rumours, like the church, find their own continuity.

So what do we make of 'The World's Biggest Problems' and the solutions put forth by:

1. 'The World's Biggest Problems' portal (web site) and its simple and clear mission of educating people all around the world about the biggest problems facing humanity.
2. The Prime Minister of the United Kingdom, David Cameron, who is offering £1 million to anyone who can solve the world's biggest problem—whatever that might be.
3. The 'Guardian Sustainable Business' professional Christian Sarkar posing the question "Can business solve the world's biggest problems by disruptive change?"
4. Real Clear Science's Alex Berezow who claims the single biggest threat facing humanity is poverty, which is neither sexy nor trendy, but nonetheless true.
5. The Christian Belief Systems and the role of the church and 5 challenges PopeFrancis will have to face as the new leader of the Roman Catholic Church.

As always, the answer is associated with 'Our Ultimate Purpose in Life', whereby the degree of our current problems is associated with the simple fact that we do not have a common denominator around the world.

This is becoming increasingly clear to us when we consider "The History of 'The Meaning of Life' so far", as illustrated in Appendix E, and the reference relating to the underlying motivation:

a) To realize one's potential and ideals
b) To achieve biological perfection
c) To seek wisdom and knowledge
d) To do good, to do the right thing
e) To meanings relating to religion
f) To love, to feel, to enjoy the act of living:
g) To have power, to be better
h) To life having no meaning

i) To know and understand the meaning of life

j) To the perception that 'Life is bad'

And whilst the human race managed to survive on the basis of the perception of reality by one and all, the accrued losses and the increase in the severity and frequency of the losses is forces us to rethink our strategy.

This takes us back to 'The Higher Ethical Plane' and 'The Quality of Mind' above all, the lack of which, or problems of the mind, may be associated with the fact that we do not yet have a science relating to their prevention.

After all, the sciences of Psychology, Psychiatry, Neurology and a myriad of other sciences and pseudo sciences relating to the problems of the mind are only designed to deal with the problems once they have occurred.

And whilst there have been many breakthroughs and prevention of the same problems in the near future, this is not going to stop us from eventually going over the edge', as illustrated earlier under 'The Fool on the Hill'.

This takes us to the social controls and the needs and expectations of the community at large, as discussed under 'Economic Policy, Environment and Resources Policy, Law and Justice Policy and Social Policy'.

That is, like the products and services of industry are only designed to deal with the problems once they have occurred, the policies are only designed to deal with the problems once they have occurred.

In that context, the prohibition of any adverse behaviour and the associated powers of the Military, or power 'over' the people concept, has lost its edge, as we can see in the history of the modern world.

On that note, let us consider a name for the missing science or "The Body of Knowledge dealing with the Quality of the Mind", which may well be represented by the acronym of "Psy—Qua—Logy' or 'Psyqualogy'.

The key to the success of the new science lies in the connection between the 'Grand Order of Design' and 'The Human Condition', whereby the degree of our problems are proportionate to the perception of reality by one and all.

In the meantime, we are either preoccupied with our own problems, disagreeing on which problem comes first, or why we should spend our hard earned money, effort and/or time on solving other people's problems.

The latter is probably the most difficult one to explain, as we saw in the illustration of 'The Fool on the Hill', according to which a large proportion of the world's population is not really hard up or living in poverty. (The World Bank estimated 1.29 billion people were living in absolute poverty in 2008)

And whilst the remaining 5.7 billion people may not be entirely immune to the problems of the world, they are nevertheless reluctant when it comes to their active contribution towards the solution of the problems.

That is, unless their personal problems become a 'Commercial Opportunity' relating to their basic need gratification and/or interaction need gratification, as illustrated below under "The Windows of Opportunity?"

The Windows of Opportunity

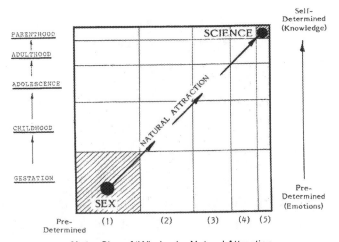

Note: Size of 'Window' = Natural Attraction

Fig.: 2.2.2

<u>Note:</u> A window of opportunity is considered '*a short time period during which an otherwise unattainable opportunity exists. After the window of opportunity closes, the opportunity ceases to exist*'.

The illustration portrays the importance of our formative years and, in some instances, the fact that a missed opportunity cannot be remedied later on, as the window may be shut permanently from there on.

The phenomenon is particularly visible in the gestation period and 'The Process of Natural Selection' relating to the chromosomes in the egg and the sperm, which are set in concrete once they are selected.

To a lesser extent, the subsequent stages and basic needs and interaction needs of the mother are bound to influence 'The Windows of Opportunity' until the child is born and afforded a degree of self-determination.

The five stages of our growth and development are indicative of 'Our Ultimate Purpose in Life' and 'The Battle of Nature & Nurture', where the gestation period is based on the knowledge of the distant past.

This is followed by our childhood which is primarily based on the knowledge of the recent past and the skills and habits of our parents and the prevailing products and services and social controls, or culture.

Our adolescence is predominantly based on our perception of reality relating to the present moment and our need to find an application for our uniqueness as a body and mind, which can be difficult for everybody.

Having been there and done that, we are now ready to apply our fitness in the realms of the businesses of industry, where the focus is predominantly on the near future and the creation of new products and services.

Finally, we may actually entertain the thought of parenthood as we focus on the distant future and the continuity of the human race and our contribution towards that objective by way of a child or two.

This brings us back to the gestation period and the development of the brain, which starts well before birth and is very important during the first three years of life as the child's experiences help wiring the brain.

At birth, a baby's brain contains 100 billion neurons, roughly as many nerve cells as there are stars in the Milky Way, and almost all the neurons the brain will ever have.

The brain starts forming prenatally, about three weeks after conception, when the brain produces trillions more neurons and "synapses" (connections between the brain cells) than it needs.

During the first years of life, the brain undergoes a series of extraordinary changes in the brain and the neurons that are there at birth, as well as some synapses, and as the neurons mature, more and more synapses are made.

At birth, the number of synapses per neuron is 2,500, but by age two or three, it's about 15,000 per neuron, and whilst the brain eliminates connections that are seldom or never used, this is a normal part of brain development.

'The Windows of Opportunity' are sensitive periods in children's lives when specific types of learning take place, and scientists have determined that the neurons for vision begin sending messages back and forth rapidly at 2 to 4 months of age, peaking in intensity at 8 months.

It is no coincidence that babies begin to take notice of the world during this period.

Scientists believe that language is acquired most easily during the first ten years of life, as the circuits in children's brains become wired for how their own language sounds.

An infant's repeated exposure to words clearly helps her brain build the neural connections that will enable him/her to learn more words later on and early stimulation sets the stage for how children will learn and interact with others throughout life.

A child's experiences, good or bad, influence the wiring of the brain and the connection in the nervous system, where loving interactions with caring adults strongly stimulate a child's brain, causing synapses to grow and existing connections to get stronger.

And whilst connections that are used become permanent, if a child receives little stimulation early on, the synapses will not develop, and the brain will make fewer connections.

Stress can become toxic when a child has frequent or prolonged experiences like abuse, neglect or poverty without adult support, yet when adults are present to support a child's experiences and help the child's stress levels, stressors may be tolerable.

Examples of tolerable stress include loss of a loved one, illness or injury, or poverty when a caring adult helps the child adapt, and some stresses are even thought of as positive stress, such as when there is a small amount of fear or sadness, or everyday challenges.

In experiences of positive stress, the system can return to a calm state in a relatively short period of time, however, when children are faced with physical or emotional stress or trauma, the hormone cortisol is released when the brain sends a signal from the hypothalamus to the adrenal cortex, which is a gland above the kidney.

High levels of cortisol can cause brain cells to die and reduces the connections between the cells in certain areas of the brain, harming the vital brain circuits, in other words, the wiring of the house can be severely damaged or miswired if a child is exposed to repeated and long-time stress without the assistance of a caring adult.

Babies with strong, positive emotional bonds to their caregivers show consistently lower levels of cortisol in their brains.

At the same time, we need to be careful with respect to the limits of the child's comfort zone, as we are inclined to give the child too much freedom too early, in which lies an error of judgement we may regret later on.

On the other hand, we may be too concerned about the health and safety of the child and, in the process, hinder the natural development of its immune system which, again, is bound to be irreparable later on.

We can allocate each window of opportunity a priority ranking based on 'The Hierarchy of Needs' from left to right, and 'The Hierarchy of Dependency' from bottom to top and the value allocation from 5 to 1.

As a result, the 'conception' or sex window of opportunity has the greatest value of 25, (5 x 5) and the fulfilment of the parent the lowest value of 1, (1 x 1) the reality of which is reflected in our diminishing natural attraction.

In the opposite dimension, our supernatural attraction is reflected in our self-determined pursuit of the great unknown, for which we may be recognized and remembered beyond our physical existence on earth.

We can associate 'The Windows of Opportunity' with the powers of Mythology and the pursuit of the great unknown, or lack of it, which begins with our interaction needs from the time of our birth onwards.

For example, the Roman Catholic Church claims that, if they can have the first seven years of a child's life, this is all they need to insure a lifelong influence, which is echoed by Napoleon stating that, as the twig is bent, so the tree will grow.

This is borne out by the many cases of children who have been lost and brought up by animals during these formative years, whereby even with the best tuition, they never learn to become a self aware personality.

And so time is a mystery to them, and even though their brain size and function is normal, they never approach the usual capabilities that education gives to modern women and men.

According to Rudolph Steiner, the great teacher of Anthroposophy, the seven-year cycles continue throughout life, and are of the utmost importance to doctors when it comes to their understanding of the body and mind.

For example, in the first seven years of our life, we pass through an incredible process of learning, which includes motor movements, speech and relationships between ourselves and the broader environment

And that means learning a vast amount about what is useful, entertaining or harmful; about what responses we get from others, and developing habits of response that may be difficult to change in later years.

The learning of language is like a powerful computer program that gives us the ability to develop an identity and self awareness as we move toward becoming an individual and learn to say "I" and know what we mean.

During this first stage of development the developing, inner forces are working to transform the body of the child from one that was inherited from the parents, to one that represents the full personality of the child.

If we do not achieve that full personality as a child, the reaction may be felt at a time of emotional stress as in the withdrawal of a partner, even if there is no sign of them withdrawing physically.

The personality aspects continue to grow during the next cycle of seven years as the concepts and association of ideas and emotions that began in the first cycle begin to be discovered by the child.

The second cycle is a time of inner expansion, as the child begins to experience and test abilities in the broader sense of the outside world, and it may learn to share and control earlier instincts in favour of group dynamics.

This takes us to is the third cycle from fourteen to twenty-one, during which we become conscious of ourselves in a new way, and with a different relationship to life—one might say we become "self conscious."

During this period, the emotional range expands in all directions as we develop a new appreciation of music, art, literature, people as well as the ability to distinguish subtler tones of colour and sound.

Besides this the average person might go through the difficult struggle of breaking away from home life and/or parental influence, which produces conflict as the person learns some degree of independence.

Also, the opposite sex, or sex as an urgent impulse, usually becomes all important as the new emotions pour in upon our personality.

Many youths experience a different relationship to religion and life's mysteries as they approach twenty-one, produce a sense of social and individual responsibility, if not a sense of a direction or life purpose.

And whilst this may not be immediately recognised, it is a time of searching for life purpose, independence, a realization of choices plus a testing of social and personal limitations as well as an awareness of one's sexuality.

All in all, the period is a time of adding maturity, dignity and poise to the person and, if these changes have not occurred by twenty-one, the person has in some way not covered the necessary aspects of development.

Because of these changes, thought should be given to early marriage, as the partner one would choose at seventeen or eighteen, is likely to be different to the partner chosen at twenty-one and beyond.

The emotional development at this age is possibly seen as initial uncertainty or clumsiness concerning emotional and sexual contact, which often involves the desire to explore many different relationships.

We are still finding out what our real needs are as the sexual drive is at full flood, whereby a partner at this point in time may be loved for ones own needs—rather than out of recognition of who the other person is.

The cycle that follows from twenty-one to twenty-eight can more or less be called a process of personality enlargement and refinement, as it is the period that we mentally and emotionally enter into adulthood.

We start to build the foundations for our careers and intimate relationships with a driving energy that we hope will gain us entry and respect in the larger world.

One of the most marked features is the developing sense of discrimination and the faculties of insight, intuition, judgement and understanding, which come to the fore as our personality softens and begins to mellow.

The sparks of interest that were awakened in the previous cycles begin to be developed along more definite lines, as the abilities of the last cycle begin to flourish and the adult emotional age emerges.

This shows as a growing sense of recognising needs of ones partner yet not denying ones own, which is followed by an ability to be something for the partner's sake without losing ones own independence or will.

We may also begin to confront the issue that we were either born with, or arose through the challenges and pains of your infancy and childhood, which usually show up in the way we handle intimate relationships.

The changes in our personality become more subtle as the years pass, where the next cycle from twenty eight to thirty-five, for instance, is one where the creative process of mind becomes most active.

Researchers and inventors make their greatest advances during these years, the evidence of which lies in the fact that the association centres of the brain come to their peak efficiency at about thirty-five years of age.

This is furthermore evident in the great teachers and philosophers who came to some vital experience at thirty-five, like Jesus, Buddha, Paul, Dante and Jacob Behmen who had their greatest insights during this period.

From the thirty-fifth to the forty-second year, some of us may begin to feel a new sense of restlessness and to some degree a desire to share whatever we have gained or lost through life with other people.

Thus we find many successful business men building libraries, or aiding colleges and the arts at this period in their life, where the aspirations of a life time can be taken to greater subtlety during this period.

This is almost like unfolding something, perhaps similar to the way a flower unfolds a bud that has been developing in earlier phases of its growth, or a fully grown tree that is producing a new season of fruit.

This is when we reassess the results of what we are doing externally in our life as in our relationships, careers, habits and the ways we interact, all of which is put under scrutiny and modified or changed.

We may even reach new heights of self-realisation and creativity not touched upon before, like the profound breakthrough of our innate genius that emerges around this time and wants to be expressed in some degree.

In the next cycle from forty-two until forty-nine a major change usually takes place, as all of our life experience up till this age is being digested and extracted in the light of new ideals and a new direction in life.

There is often tremendous unrest in this period and that following it, as the unlived aspects of life cry out to be recognised and allowed, and the desire to make a mark in life is pressing upon our sense of urgency.

At this point it appears to many of us that we have reached the mid point of our life and from here on there will be a decline, and even if this is not so, it is often felt very strongly and acted upon in one way of another.

For example, people may change partners, life directions, and even attempt major personal changes, although these latter may have begun in the last cycle.

Also, the emotional age and maturing of love may at last show some signs of a lasting and unconditional love which, if it has not already appeared to some degree, might be one that is still locked in the earlier stages.

Many maintain the emotional age of a child right into the mature years, as they feel all the fear of abandonment, jealousy and possessiveness of childhood leading to divorces and new directions around this period.

In these years we move from old stereotypical roles to a new found confidence in our individuality, as we are prepared to please our self rather than society and gain a real understanding of our uniqueness.

This brings us to the Johari Window model and simple tool for improving self-awareness and mutual understanding between individuals within a group and to improve the group's relationship with other groups.

There are two key ideas behind the tool:

1. That we can build trust with others by disclosing information about ourselves.
2. That, with the help of feedback from others, we can learn about ourselves and come to terms with personal issues.

By explaining the idea of the Johari Window, we can help team members to understand the value of self-disclosure, and we can encourage them to give, and accept, constructive feedback.

Done sensitively, this can help people build better, more trusting relationships with one another, solve issues, and work more effectively as a team.

The model was devised by American psychologists Joseph Luft and Harry Ingham in 1955, while researching group dynamics at the University of California Los Angeles, covering a four-quadrant grid, whereby:

1. The Open Area (Quadrant 1)

This quadrant represents the things that we know about ourselves, and the things that others know about us. This includes our behaviour, knowledge, skills, attitudes, and "public" history.

2. The Blind Area (Quadrant 2)

This quadrant represents things about us that we aren't aware of, but are known by others.

This can include simple information that we do not know, or it can involve deep issues (for example, feelings of inadequacy, incompetence, unworthiness, or rejection), which are often difficult for individuals to face directly, and yet can be seen by others.

3. The Hidden Area (Quadrant 3)

This quadrant represents things that we know about ourselves, but that others don't know.

4. The Unknown Area (Quadrant 4)

This last quadrant represents things that are unknown by us, and are unknown by others.

The ultimate goal of the Johari Window is to enlarge the Open Area, without disclosing information that is too personal.

The Open Area is the most important quadrant, as the more people know about each other, the more productive, cooperative, and effective they'll be when working together.

The process of enlarging the Open Area quadrant is called "self-disclosure," and it's a give-and-take process that takes place between ourselves and the people that we interact with.

As we share information, our Open Area expands vertically and our Hidden Area gets smaller, and as people on our team provide feedback to us about what they know or see about us, our Open Area expands horizontally, and our Blind Area gets smaller.

Done well, the process of give and take, sharing, and open communication builds trust within the group.

The Johari Window may look complex, but it's actually easy to understand with a little effort, as it provides a visual reference that people can use to look at their own character, whilst illustrating the importance of sharing, being open, and accepting feedback from others.

People who have a large Open Area are usually very easy to talk to, they communicate honestly and openly with others, and they get along well with a group.

People who have a very small Open Area are difficult to talk to, they seem closed off and uncommunicative, and they often don't work well with others, because they're not trusted.

Other people might have a large Blind Area, with many issues that they haven't identified or dealt with yet. However, others can see these issues clearly. These people might have low self-esteem, or they may even have anger issues when working with others.

This brings us back to 'Our Ultimate Purpose in Life' and the proposition that the degree of our problems at any one time is proportionate to "The Perception of Reality" by one and all, as illustrated below.

Hans-Juergen Strichow

The Perception of Reality

Stage	Concepts of Life	Perception by	Basic Need
1	Unknown & Incomprehensible	Impact on Community	Fulfillment Need
2	Unknown but Comprehensible	Impact on Others	Esteem Need
3	Unknown but Imaginable	Impact on Individual	Social Need
4	Little Known but Comparable	Similar Experiences	Safety Need
5	Known & Measurable	Percentage Accuracy	Survival Need

Fig.: 2.2.3

The illustration is portraying the pursuit of the great unknown from the 'unknown & incomprehensible' concepts of life and their 'impact on the community' at large to the 'known & measurable' concepts.

The stages 1 to 5 represent the basic needs in a reverse order, beginning with the fulfillment seekers considering the acquisition of a greater fitness and contribution towards 'Our Ultimate Purpose in Life'.

This is followed by the esteem seekers looking for a challenge, which is likely to be followed by the development of an expertise and possibly a product or a service for which there is a need in the community.

In doing so, the product or service can now be appreciated by the market on the basis of its 'value for money' and the associated 'impact on the individual', which is by no means a foregone conclusion.

This includes the uniqueness of the body and the mind, in which case the marginal groups or individuals may not represent a 'Commercial Opportunity' unless they become a burden or nuisance value to society.

Having acquired the product or service, we can now compare its value against 'similar experiences' in the recent past, and if it does not compare favorably, we are likely to have a problem with our purchase.

If the outcome is positive, we are likely to add to our existing fitness for purpose, whereby the 'known & measurable' benefits may even be filtered through to our genes if they are deemed to be 'stable & predictable'.

And so the pendulum swings in the other direction as we are bound to protect our newly acquired fitness before seeking an application and applying our fitness as an expression of our emerging esteem need.

In that context, 'The Perception of Reality' is also reversed, as our newly acquired fitness is now based on the 'percentage efficiency' of our survival needs and the protection of that fitness on 'similar experiences', etc.

And so "The Survival of the Fittest" works its way from the bottom up, whilst "The Survival of the Fairest" is working its way from the top down, in which lies also the principles underlying "The Battle of Nature & Nurture".

All going well, the forces of Nurture will eventually triumph over the forces of Nature, upon which we would have reached the pinnacle of our existence here on earth and readiness to continue our journey as a child of the universe.

From a scientific perspective, the five stages represent the pursuit of the great unknown from the development of a Pseudoscience to its 'percentage accuracy' relating to a scientific method of measurement.

Note: While the standards for determining whether a body of knowledge, method or practice is scientific can vary from field to field, a number of basic principles are widely agreed upon by the scientific community.

The aim is that all experimental results should be reproducible under the same conditions and verifiable by others, allowing further investigation to determine whether a hypothesis is both valid and reliable.

Standards require the scientific method to be applied throughout, and bias will be controlled for, or eliminated through, randomization, fair sampling procedures, blinding of studies, and other methods of validation.

All gathered data, including the experimental or environmental conditions, are expected to be documented for scrutiny and made available for peer review, allowing further experiments or studies to be conducted.

Statistical quantification of significance, confidence and error are also important tools for the scientific method.

One such 'Pseudoscience' or service is the 'Conversion Therapy' which seeks to change a non-heterosexual person's sexual orientation so that they will no longer be homosexual or similar gender confusion.

The American Psychiatric Association has condemned the psychiatric treatment such as reparative or conversion therapy which is ultimately based on the assumption that homosexuality is a mental disorder.

It states that, "Ethical practitioners should refrain from attempts to change individuals' sexual orientation by calling into question the motives and even the character of the individuals on both sides of the issue.

It also states that political and moral debates over the integration of gays and lesbians into the mainstream of American society have obscured scientific data about changing sexual orientation in general."

On that note, we may want to consider the 'Pseudoscience' in the light of the Christian belief system and 'The Power of Prayer', as the two phenomena are intertwined within the mind cycle and mind growth.

For example, according to the *Washington Post*, prayer is the most common complement to mainstream medicine and far outpacing acupuncture, herbs, vitamins and other alternative remedies of today."

Yet he largest and most scientifically rigorous study found no significant difference whether subjects were prayed for or not, except some negative effects among those who knew they were receiving prayers.

On the issue of praying on behalf of others, Christian teachings have emphasized the need for guidance from the 'Holy Spirit' as to what needs to be prayed for and have taught that "God" can not be coerced.

The philosophical controversy on this topic even involves the basic issues of statistical inference and ability to "prove" or "disprove" something, and whether this topic is even within the realm of science at all.

In comparison to other fields that have been scientifically studied, carefully monitored studies of prayer are relatively few, and the field remains tiny with about $5 million spent worldwide on such research each year.

So how does this fit in with our 'comprehensibility' proposition, whereby everything in the universe follows laws, without exception?

To begin with, we have to differentiate between the 'prayer' and the 'prayee' or person being prayed, whereby the 'prayer' is supported by the 'SOUL' in direct proportion to his or her belief or 'powers of conviction'.

Under the circumstances, the prayer is going to be issued with an energy relating to 'its' imagined expectations of a potential gain, and so it is increasing his or her chances of success on a personal level.

This would explain the findings of the *Washington Post,* which is not about giving other people a metaphysical medicine, but rather self inducing that medicine with seemingly astounding effects.

And every time the medicine is delivered and working on behalf of that person, the belief is reinforced and strengthened as the individual is pursuing the great unknown relating to our metaphysical dimension.

At the same time, the praying on behalf of other people is having a mixed effect, which may be due partly to the prayees's lack of awareness of the fact, and partly to its powers of conviction, or lack thereof.

And so we come to the conclusion that 'The Power of Conviction' or 'Imagined Expectations of a Potential Gain' or 'The Prevention of a Potential Loss' are ultimately behind the power of prayer, or the lack thereof.

By the same token, this reality would not help the belief systems simply because it would remove their powers 'over' the minds, and so they bury their heads in the sand as they feed on the naivety of the followers.

Does this make the participating belief systems good or evil, and do the followers get a chance to be reincarnated in another body when they have really failed to pursue 'Our Ultimate Purpose in Life'?

In the same vein, are the people with inherited or acquired diseases of the body or the mind good or bad, simply because they don't meet 'our' expectation in life?

In reality, there is no such thing as good or evil diseases of the body or the mind due to the simple fact that 'without the element of bad, we wouldn't know the element of good', in which lies the philosophy of life.

Other Pseudosciences can be found in Astronomy, Divination, Earth & Earth Sciences, Paranormal & Ufology, Psychology, Health & Medicine, Religious & Spiritual Beliefs, Physics, (Theories & Energies) Products, (Value) Racial Theories, Idiosyncratic Ideas and many others.

Note: An idiosyncrasy is an unusual feature of a person which includes odd habits.

Idiosyncrasy defined the way physicians conceived diseases in the 19th century, as they considered each disease of the body and the mind as a unique condition relating to the makeup of a patient.

This began to change in the 1870s when discoveries by researchers in Europe permitted the advent of a 'scientific medicine', a precursor to the 'Evidence-Based Medicine' that is the standard of practice today.

<u>Note:</u> *Evidence-based medicine (EBM) was subsequently extended to evidence-based health care (EBHC) or Evidence-based practice (EBP) so as to broaden its application to allied health care professionals.*

Evidence-based medicine, health care and practices have been defined as *"the conscientious, explicit and judicious use of current best evidence in making decisions about the care of individual patients."*

Or more specifically, *"the use of mathematical estimates of benefits and harm, derived from high-quality research on population samples so as to facilitate the diagnosis, investigation and management of patients."*

A similar push for the use of scientific practices happened in the 1970 when the Japanese manufacturing industries began to experience major problems with the quality of their products around the world.

In order to resolve the problem, they employed the services of American statisticians like Dr. Edward Deming and Walter A. Shewhart who is known for his 'Control Charts' to determine if a process is in 'statistical control'.

The control aspect lies in a) the 'stable & predictable' variability of the characteristic being observed, and b) the average and the width of the (bell shaped) distribution and its comparison against the given limits.

The concept is not unlike 'The Forces of Nature & Nurture' as the control chart is designed to prevent the process from exceeding the given limits, tolerance, or 'Comfort Zone' having been specified on the drawing.

In the final analysis, the process and/or product characteristics were sorted into:

1. the 'stable & predictable' patterns that may need to be inspected periodically,
2. the 'unstable but predictable' patterns that could be addressed with skills and habits,

3. the 'unstable & unpredictable' patterns that required the constant attention of the operator.

Another statistician is Dr. Joseph M. Juran who revolutionized the Japanese philosophy on quality management, and in no small way worked to help shape their economy into the industrial leader it is today.

Dr. Juran was the first to incorporate the human aspect of quality management often referred to as Total Quality Management, which involved top management and the need for widespread training in quality.

And the trend didn't stop there, as we can see in the ever-increasing demand for a scientific approach relating to the management of the needs and expectations of the businesses of industry and the stakeholders alike.

On that note, let us begin with the 'Uses and Gratifications Theory' (UGT) which is a scientific approach to understanding why and how people actively seek out specific media to satisfy specific needs.

The UGT is a consequence of our need gratification in a 'consumerism' society, where many people tend to formulate their goals in life partly through acquiring goods that they clearly do not need for subsistence.

In doing so, they become enmeshed in the process of acquisition or shopping, as they take some of their identity from a possession of new items that they buy as an expression of their social status in life.

In that context, UGT is an audience based approach to understanding mass communication and the question of "what do people do with the media", rather than the question of "what does the media do to people".

It assumes that audience members are not passive consumers of media but rather that the audience has power over their media consumption and assumes an active role in interpreting and integrating media into their own lives.

UGT holds the view that audiences are responsible for choosing a media to meet their desires and needs to achieve gratification, which would then imply that the media compete against other information sources.

In doing so, the media is working with 'The Perception of Reality' ranging from the 'unknown & incomprehensible' to the 'known & measurable' product characteristics as it advertises the industry's products and services.

2.3　The Natural Personalities

This brings us to the basic need gratification and 'The Windows of Opportunity' relating to our imagined expectations of a potential gain or a loss from the time of our conception to the time of our natural death.

As to our gestation period, the opportunities are obviously associated with the needs and expectations of our mother and the prevailing culture, in which case we have very little control over the matter.

This is about to change from our birth onwards, as we convey our specific needs and expectations reflecting our uniqueness as a body and mind, as illustrated below under "The Basic Need Gratification".

The Basic Need Gratification

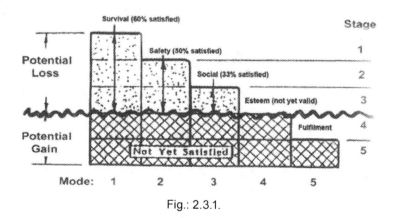

Fig.: 2.3.1.

The illustration portrays the forces of Nature and our predetermined mental capacity and behaviour relating to our progressive conscious awareness of our survival, safety, social, esteem and fulfillment needs.

Whilst the illustration represents the opposite to the illustration entitled 'The New World Order', the dynamics relating to "The Survival of the Fittest" are identical to those of "The Survival of the Fairest".

That is, just like we allocated a value from 5 to 1 to the social controls, the basic needs may be given a value from 5 to 1, which stands for our need to survive, be safe, belong, be valued and be fulfilled, respectively.

And so the acquisition of a 20% 'fitness for purpose' is now opening the door for stage 2, whereby the 80% x 5 = 4 potential fitness gains are met by a 100% x 4 = 4 potential protection gains.

The principle continues as we manage to satisfy our basic needs, whereby the 60% x 5 = 3 potential survival gains are met by a 75% x 4 = 3 potential safety and a 100% x 3 = 3 potential social gains.

In that context, the illustration is showing us at an even potential gains level for the survival, safety, social and esteem needs, upon which our focus may shift towards our 'Want to Compete' with other others.

In the physical sense, this could mean our instinctive desire to compete with other males/females as we express our esteem needs relating to the survival of the species and the right to continue our genes.

If we prove ourselves equal or better than others, we may even progress towards the satisfaction of our fulfilment or actualization needs as we compete for the top position within the social hierarchy.

A similar concept applies to the businesses of industry and government and 'The Basic Need Gratification' in our role as a customer, supplier, employee, shareholder and the community at large.

In that context, let us apply the above to our place of employment and our attitude and behaviour towards the management, where we are frequently told to "Shut up and do as you are told", that is until we left.

The reason for doing so was more associated with our interaction needs and frustration with the management style than the adequacy of our wages and conditions, which were more than the average at the time.

To be specific, we were at stage 5 of our personal growth and development, and so we were expressing our needs and expectations in the entire need spectrum, as illustrated below under "The Situation Analysis".

The Situation Analysis

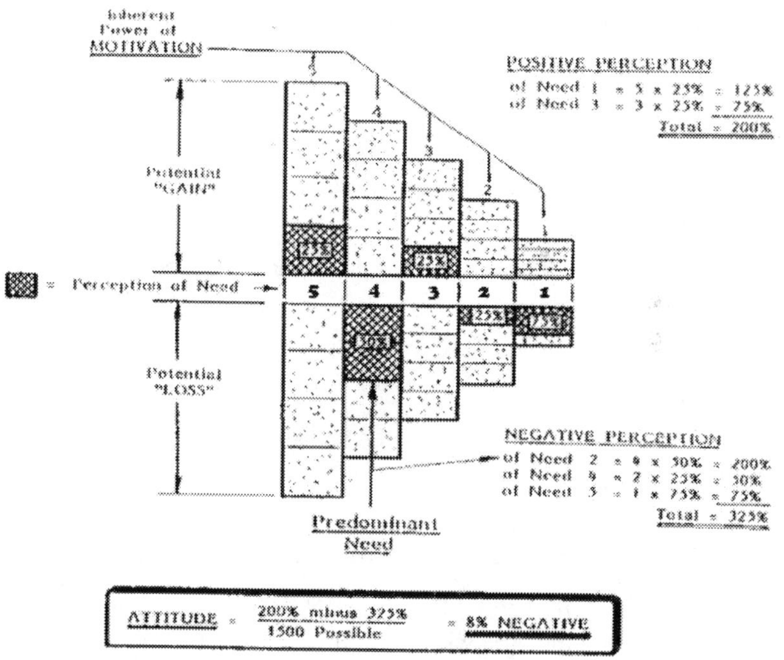

Fig.: 2.3.2

In that context, the attitude is showing our perception of a 200% potential gain versus a 325% potential loss over 1,500% maximum possible in the positive or negative dimension = 8% negative attitude.

If someone was to ask us about our feelings relating to the situation in hand, we would probably direct our 'selective attention' towards our perceived lack of job security, which is not to say we are correct.

By the same token, the analysis is allowing us to evaluate the situation with respect to our 'predominant need' or greatest problem which may then be resolved with the help of a mediator or trained facilitator.

If the mediator manages to resolve the safety problem to a passive value, our 8% negative attitude may become a 5% positive attitude reflecting the pos. 200% minus neg. 125% = 75% over 1,500% possible.

As it happens, the customer does not think in terms of its basic needs in the short and long term, but rather in terms of the affordability, safety, function, appearance and service of the product or service, whereby:

1) survival = 5 for 'Affordability' = the cost of acquisition, installation and maintenance
2) safety = 4 for 'Safety' = the prevention of a short, medium or longer term harm
3) social = 3 for 'Function' = the performance criteria, their reliability and durability
4) esteem = 2 for 'Appearance' = the product appeal in the short, medium & long term
5) fulfillment = 1 for 'Service' = the assistance before, during and after the sale

The product criteria or customer perception of value for money is reflecting the dichotomy of 'The Quantity of Life' and 'The Quality of Life' considerations and thus the widening gap between the rich and the poor.

And whilst this does not necessarily mean that money always equates to a quality of life, the principle is clear, as we can see in the aspirations of the poor and their frequent envy and adoration of the rich and famous.

In reality, the acquisition of money is not an end in itself unless 'the acquired fitness is applied to a meaningful purpose', like the needs and expectations of the stakeholders, in which lies the key to happiness.

In doing so, the widening gap between the rich and the poor is bound to come to a halt before closing in and eventually disappearing altogether as the human race is approaching the pinnacle of its existence.

By the same token, the power of Morality will prevail as the preferred model of social control, where the 'MAPS for the Future' will render us a 'stable & predictable' Team Spirit, Team_Effort and Quality of Life.

Note: The Hierarchy of Needs is reflected in the descending values from 5 to 1 representing our survival and fulfillment needs, the latter of which could not be satisfied if there was a general lack of service.

'The Hierarchy of Needs' (Abraham Maslow) can be further weighted with a factor of 3, 2 and 1 so as to accommodate the short, medium and long term needs and expectations of the customer or market.

As a consequence, the affordability of the product in the short term (i.e. cost of acquisition) is $5 \times 3 = 15$, the cost of installation is $5 \times 2 = 10$ and the cost of application $5 \times 1 = 5$, and the same applies to the rest.

The element of fairness comes into play if the customer is not given a choice relating to the supply of a given product, in which case the customer may have a negative attitude towards the business practices.

Under the circumstances, the customer may walk away from a perfectly good product simply because he or she was treated with contempt or a myriad of other deprivations of his or her interaction needs.

If we apply the first three product criteria to the customer's perception of value for money, we may get a better picture of his/her attitude towards a product, as illustrated below under "The Perception of Value for Money".

The Perception of Value for Money

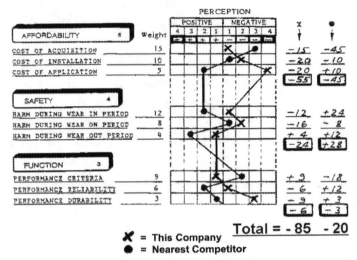

Total = - 85   - 20

✗ = **This Company**
● = **Nearest Competitor**

This Company: Neg. 30% (Cost of Installation/Application are biggest problems)

Competitor: Neg. 7% (Cost of Acquisition is single greatest problem)

Perception: 1 = 25%, 2 = 50%, 3 = 75%, 4 = 100%

Fig.: 2.3.3

The illustration is portraying this company versus its nearest competitor, in which case both have their good and bad points, which makes it difficult for us to decide which is better, and whether any one is good enough.

To start with, we are somewhat negative about both products, whereby our attitude ranges from a negative 7% for the competitor's product' to a whopping negative 30% for this company's product.

As it happened, this company seemed to be promoting the good features of the product whilst attempting to hide the bad features, the purpose of which is obviously to deceive us in our perception of reality.

If we manage to get to the bottom of it all, we are likely to reject one product on the basis of its 'perceived' excessive installation and application cost, and the other on the basis of its high cost of acquisition.

By the same token, if we had plenty of money, the affordability of the product may not actually come into our consideration as we are looking at the appearance aspects of the product above all others.

This brings us back to 'The Human Organization' and the importance of 'The Management Aspirations' relating to the customer support for the business and the 'Need to Change' its perception of reality.

In that context, the 'Need to Change' or 'Want to Compete' is ultimately based on the statistical analysis of the market and the average customer perception of a given product characteristics, whereby:

1. A negative 'Comparison' against the competitor is an Actual Problem
2. A negative 'Attitude' towards 'this' company's is an Actual Problem.
3. An individual negative 'Value' represents a Potential Problem.
4. A passive 'Value' represents a Potential Improvement.
5. A less than optimum 'Value' represents a Challenge.

On the other hand, this company (or both) may already be fully aware of its strengths and weaknesses of its products, but reluctant to invest in the research and development of a new and exciting alternative.

And so they may embark on a strategy of 'feeding on the naivety of the stakeholders', one and all or, if the stakeholders are too smart for that, they may try to 'feed on the weaknesses of the stakeholders' instead.

Whilst 'The Perception of Value for Money' may not be 100% accurate, it is nevertheless allowing us to derive at a 'known & measurable' attitude which can then be further addressed by its '% efficiency'.

On that note, let us have a closer look at the preconditioning of the mind with respect to its

'Desire + Ability + Opportunity = Behaviour to Suit' the basic need gratification process from the time of our conception onwards.

'The Behaviour to Suit' is not associated with the automatic reflexes manifested in our genes, nor does it represent our acquired skills and habits, but rather a type of 'natural' preconditioning for life.

That is, the growing mental capacity of the human mind and its need to communicate at an increasingly complex level of interaction has led to the creation of a network of muscles in our face above all.

The phenomenon is obviously associated with the forces of Nature, where every basic need and interaction need has a unique body language and behaviour, as illustrated below under "The Natural Personalities"

The Natural Personalities

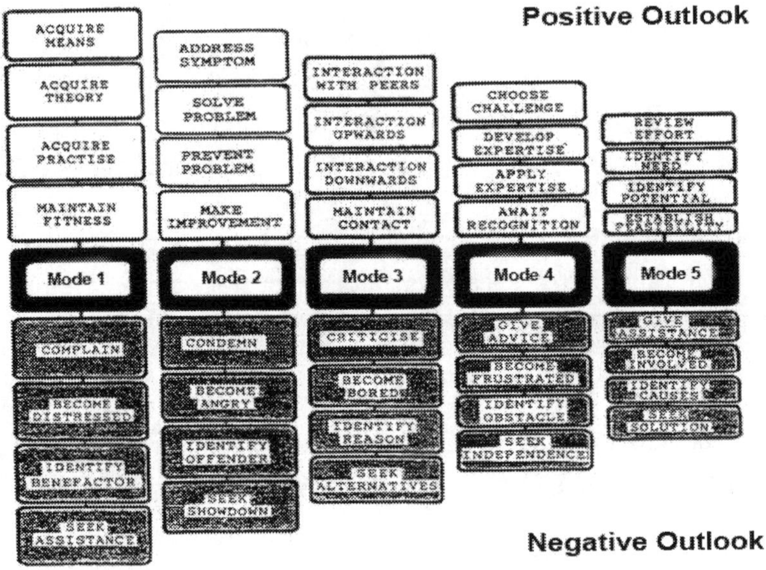

Fig.: 2.3.4

Under the circumstances, our behaviour may be associated with our blood pressure which is causing us to become angry when there is no logical reason or explanation, and so we are compelled to find out more.

If we go back to 'The Situation Analysis' and our 8% negative attitude towards the business which is largely due to the 50% negative perception of our job security, then our behaviour is likely to reflect that priority.

The patterns resemble 'The Basic Need Gratification' and the progressive top down behaviour which is repeated throughout our gestation, childhood, adolescence, adulthood and parenthood.

As a consequence, the opportunity to get married or to have sex during childhood is not going to fuel our imagination of a potential gain, as we rather spend our valuable time playing childish games.

This brings us to the possibility of a sustained negative outlook and need to seek assistance in mode 1, a showdown in mode 2, alternatives in mode 3, our independence in mode 4 and a solution in mode 5'.

Under the circumstances, the symptoms may be related to our basic needs, our interaction needs, or both, as we may discover when we are being told that our job is in doubt because we are looking for another job.

The problem is exacerbated if we are unable to 1. find the right assistance, 2. resolve the matter in a showdown, 3. find a suitable alternative, 4. manage to become independent or 5. find the right solution.

The patterns of behaviour represent a 'Social Nervous System' that is not unlike our own internal nervous system, the logic of which lies in the phenomenon of "The Mode Compatibility", as illustrated below.

The Mode Compatibility

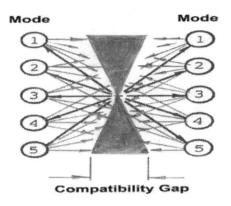

Fig.: 2.3.5

'The Mode Compatibility' represents the principle of an 'Immune System' that applies to the protection of the cells and organs as it does to any other situation of mutual dependency, organism or ecosystem.

Under the circumstances, the objective of the mode compatibility is to ensure the integrity of the whole, whereby the energy flow is regulating the nutrient cycle of the organism so as to maintain the homeostasis.

Note: In simple terms, 'Homeostasis' is a process in which the body's internal environment is kept stable, whereby multiple equilibrium adjustments and regulation mechanisms make homeostasis possible.

The optimum balance can be seen in the compatibility between modes (5) + (1), (4) + (2) and (3) + (3) or fulfillment need and survival need, esteem need and safety need, and social need and social need.

Likewise, the worst case scenario can be seen in the 'incompatibility' between modes (1) and (1) and (5) and (5), as we can see in the expression of 'The blind leading the blind' and similar popular phrases.

In order to illustrate the phenomenon of 'The Mode Compatibility':

1. Let us assume mode (1) is in need of some assistance and cannot get any, and so mode (5) may give assistance before becoming involved as an expression of its fulfillment needs.

2. The problem affecting mode (2) may well represent a challenge to mode (4), and so it may develop an expertise before applying the newly acquired skill and awaiting some recognition.

3. Finally, there is the compatibility between mode (3) and (3), both of which are looking for an opportunity to apply their fitness to a purpose, and so they get together to compare notes.

'The Mode Compatibility' is based on a mathematical formula, whereby the optimum compatibility is represented by the average of 3 as in (5+1) over 2 = 3, (4+2) over 2 = 3 and (3+3) over 2 = 3.

The worst case can be seen in a) the lack of compatibility between modes (1) + (1) and their desire to acquire a fitness for purpose, and b) the lack of compatibility between modes (5) + (5) considering a greater fitness.

For example, we may be in mode 1 and ask another mode 1 how to do something, upon which we receive a negative answer, and so we continue our search until we find a mode 5 who is happy to assist us.

On the other hand, the first person may recognize us and begin to ask questions with respect to our identity and the common denominator relating to our children or place of work, as we both move into mode 3.

The 'Opportunity' may lead to all sorts of need gratification relating to our social needs and our sense belonging as we are focusing on our need to 'Maintain Contact' with our recent past and the people thereof.

'The Mode Compatibility' is ultimately based on the interaction needs of the individuals involved, whereby:

- Only 7% of meaning is in the words spoken
- 38% of meaning is the way that the words are said
- 55% is in facial expression. (source: Albert Mehrabian)

These 'perceptions of reality' are mainly based on our mental capacity having been acquired during our previous life experiences, which is now being applied and tested in the context of 'The Ritual of Life & Death'.

'The Mode Compatibility' can also be seen in the Transactional Analysis (TA) integrative approach to the theory of psychology and psychotherapy because it has elements of psychoanalytic, humanist and cognitive approaches.

'TA' was first developed by Canadian-born US psychiatrist Eric Berne in the late 1950s in the form of the 'Parent—Adult—Child' interaction model, whereby:

1. The Parent is our 'Taught' concept of life
2. The Adult is our 'Thought' concept of life
3. The Child is our 'Felt' concept of life

The model has four positions reflecting the mode compatibility model, whereby:

1. I'm OK and you're OK—is the healthiest position about life and it means that I feel good about myself and all others in my presence.
2. I'm OK but you are not—is a position where I feel good about life but others appear not OK or less than is considered as healthy.
3. I'm not OK but you are OK—is a position where I may consider myself the weaker partner in a relationship and thus tolerate abuse.
4. I'm not OK and you are not OK—is the worst position to be in as I believe I am in a bad state, and so is the rest of the world.

The Transactional Analysis is a theory of communication that can be used to analyse systems and organizations, whilst offering a theory for child development by explaining how our adult patterns of life originated in childhood.

This explanation is based on the idea of a "Life Script"—the assumption that we continue to re-play childhood strategies, even when this results in pain or defeat, in which case it may be useful:

a) In practical application, as it can be used in the diagnosis and treatment of many types of psychological disorders and provides a method of therapy for individuals, couples, families and groups.

b) Outside the therapeutic field in education to help teachers remain in clear communication at an appropriate level, in counselling and consultancy, in management and communications training.

The 'TA' is a reflection of 'The Battle of Nature & Nurture', whereby the Parent and 'Taught' concept of life represent the recent past and the role of the 'SOUL' and our subconsciously contrived skills and habits.

Likewise, the Adult and 'Thought' concept of life represent the present and the role of the 'MIND' with respect to prevailing opportunities for the realization of a potential gain or the prevention of a potential loss.

Finally, the Child and 'Felt' concept of life has to do with 'Our Ultimate Purpose in Life', as the 'Seeker of Eternal Life & Fulfillment' (SELF) is leaving us with a life long curiosity relating to the great unknown.

'The Transaction Analysis' is something that we all know about intuitively, like when someone makes eye contact with us and gives us a warm smile, upon which the Social Nervous System is engaged.

We may feel a pleasant sensation in our face and our body and perhaps smile back as we are feeling an increase in the pleasant sensations.

In another situation, we may be having a challenging day and a colleague at work says, "It is hard sometimes, isn't it?" upon which we feel acknowledged and met in a way that speaks to the way we are feeling.

And then one of your kids is upset because someone at school said something unkind and untrue about them, and so without saying anything, we just walk over and put a hand on the child's shoulder or back.

And as they keep telling us their story and we just listen, we can see them slowly relaxing and slowing down.

Whilst 'The Mode Compatibility' has been around ever since the advent of people, it has only been in the last 10-15 years that science has identified the nerves that help us feel bonded, acknowledged, and secure.

These nerves are called the Cranial Nerves and they are known to weaken or destroy the strength or vitality of the eyes, ears, nose, mouth, face and hands, or nerves we use to see, hear, smell, taste and touch.

Some researchers, such as Dr. Stephen Porges, have realized that this special nerve network serves a critical function for us, as it helps us to regulate our autonomic (or automatic) nervous system.

It especially helps that nervous system to discharge any sense of threat, danger or stress that we feel, whereby this Social Nervous System is probably our most elegant and efficient means of relieving stress.

This nervous system is a critical part of our very first experiences in life, at birth and in the days and weeks after birth, and if a child has a fairly stress-free birth, it will appear radiant and attractive to its parents.

And so they will be powerfully attracted to the child, and it will fall in love and bond with them, and thus ensure that it will have secure attachment that will help it be nurtured and protected through its early years.

Research has shown that newborns who become securely attached feel welcomed and comfortable in the world, as they go through their developmental steps in a much easier and progressive way than others.

The secure attachment enables them also to trust and rely on their own Social Nervous Systems throughout their lives as their primary way to cope with stress, life challenges and relationship to the hearts.

And whilst our hearts have long been seen to be the organs which pump blood throughout our bodies, we now know that our hearts are really not capable of moving blood through the miles of arteries and veins

That is, the heart has a moderate pumping action which is only enough to get blood started in its circulatory routing, whereas the motility of the body's energy system is what facilitates the full movement of blood.

What our hearts do even more extraordinary than the blood-pumping function is the fact that the heart has the largest energy field of any part of our body, a field that extends up to 30 feet out in front of our bodies.

With its huge energy field, the heart is the primary modulator of incoming and outgoing energy for the body as it reflects the expressions of our emotional status such as love, warmth, caring and nurturing, etc.

As it stands, 'The Social Nervous System' is no longer a personal issue as we are now exposed to the Internet and means of communication that is the foundation of society, business and government.

There are now at least 1.6 billions of us connected via computer and 3 billion mobile devices that touch the Internet, including the rise of "social" technologies—such as wikis, blogs, Twitter, SMS and social networks.

As more and more people get connected, we see an acceleration in the way the Internet is used to coordinate action and render services such as 'Emergency Responses', 'Political Action' and 'Global Forecasting'.

The social nervous system makes us aware of a broader context of relationship with humanity, as our immediate relationships with our family, our city and our state begins to span the entire globe.

Using 'The Social Nervous System', we are finding solutions to some big problems such as controlling diseases or responding to emergencies followed by a feedback that exposes the actions of a powerful few to the many.

It is no coincidence that "transparency" is a catch phrase in government and business these days, as it is a natural by-product of the emerging Social Nervous System that engenders a healthier balance of power in society.

Another outcome of the social nervous system is that we see the shift away from privacy as an inalienable right to an individual responsibility, as we are witnessing increasing pressure to be connected to Facebook, Twitter and so on.

Whilst those who do not connect, share and collaborate will have a hard time in business and in social life, older generations expect that digital natives will one day wish to erase all their indiscreet photos online.

And whilst the complexity of the modern world and getting people to reach out and touch their neighbours is a good thing, it will come at the price of reshaping our identities as part of a larger, interconnected whole.

2.4   The Higher Personalities

This brings us to the 'Higher Personalities' and our cosmic connection in the form of 'The Process of Supernatural Selection', according to which only the most suitable minds are reinstated in another life.

It may be impossible for us to ascertain the exact criteria relating to our potential reincarnation in another life, especially when we consider the symptom bearers are just as important as the solution seekers.

'The Higher Personalities' represent the forces of Nurture and our predetermined mental capacity and behaviour relating to the ongoing creation of new and exciting products and services and social controls.

The cosmic connection can be seen in the personality traits attributed to the Zodiac belt or circle around which our luminescent Sun apparently moves month by month throughout the calendar year.

The word Zodiac literally means animals and refers to the patterns of creatures seen in the stars that apparently transmit the energy of the different constellational signs or the celestial radiations to our planet earth.

And whilst there is much debate about the validity of that theory, and in particular the detailed nature of our personality traits relating to a given date and time of birth, there appears to be some correlation.

Furthermore, we cannot deny our different personality traits which are not associated with our parents and/or our inherited genes, nor can they be associated with our culture and our acquired skills and habits.

Under the circumstances, our personality traits relating to the Zodiac or some other extraterrestrial influence can only be associated with the fertilization and the subsequent growth of the cosmic foetus.

And now we have another problem relating to the Zodiac and its association with the date of birth, in which case our personality traits began with the fertilization of the cosmic fetus and not the birth of the child.

And so it is only natural to assume our higher personalities begin with the fertilization of the human egg, upon which the left and right brain functions are increasingly expressing their powers of self-determination.

The left brainers can be seen in their desire to use logic in place of feelings and to focus on details, whereas the right brainers focus on the big picture with imagination and feelings relating to the great unknown.

The right brain is the key to all the great inventors, writers, artists and composers in the history of man, none of which would have been possible without the intense study of our universe, or Astrology.

That is, Astrology is the study of correlations of celestial events with behaviour on earth, particularly correlations which cannot be explained by gravitation, magnetism or other forces associated with physics.

The Zodiac is known to have been in use by the Roman era, based on concepts inherited by Hellenistic astronomy from Babylonian astronomy of the Chaldean period. (mid-1st millennium BC)

Although the Zodiac remains the basis of the ecliptic coordinate system in use in astronomy besides the equatorial one, the term and the names of the twelve signs are today mostly associated with the Horoscope.

In that context, "The Higher Personalities" may be divided into 4 groups which are triggered in the reverse order to our 'Basic Personalities', whereby mode 4 = Group 1 and mode 3 = Group 2 etc., as illustrated below.

The Higher Personalities

Fig.: 2.4.1

That is, the personality traits of 'Group One' represent the typical behaviour associated with Mode 4, 'Group Two' with Mode 3, 'Group Three' with Mode 2 and 'Group Four' with Mode 1.

Each group is further divided into C = Cardinal, F = Fixed and M = Mutable aspects of behaviour, which is designed to reinforce the specific purpose of each group, whereby:

The Cardinal Signs (Aries, Cancer, Libra and Capricorn) are rather passionate about getting things moving, as they want to use their abilities without delay.

The Fixed Signs (Taurus, Leo, Sagittarius and Pisces) can be relied upon to build with dogged persistence, as they want to stabilize assets and never give up.

The Mutable Signs (Gemini, Virgo, Scorpio and Aquarius) are versatile and flexible in every new situation, as they want to adapt to conditions and like variety.

Whilst each star sign has its own set of personality traits, the Cardinal, Fixed and Mutable aspects of their behaviour are only significant in the context of a team effort or team spirit, whereby:

Group 1 people show an enthusiasm for life, and their energy is prodigious where initiating projects is concerned, which is aided by their ability to survive and adapt.

Group 1 people also tend to share what they think, create and produce, and they are in need of fairly constant appreciation and approval for what they do, more than those of the other modes.

The desire to be free characterizes many of their belongings, and they may not react well to having restrictions imposed on them, considering they need to grow and make their mark in the world.

<u>Group 2</u> people have more measured responses than group 1 people, are more critical and their energies are a bit less focused on initiating projects and more on bringing them to fruition.

Group 2 people also tends to be a mixture of introvert and extrovert, where emphatic urges to become involved with others are strong and feelings play an more important role in colouring their lives

They may not display an overwhelming need to bring their contributions out in the world, and many hidden characteristics develop at this time whilst being appreciated is not always the most important thing.

<u>Group 3</u> people demonstrate both a greater ability and need to control their external environment and so they are rarely as enthusiastic as those belonging to group 1 and 2, being rather more selective and critical.

Whilst feelings are kept under stricter control, social urges are more maturely and fully expressed here also, where friendships, group and community activities and direct working contributions to society are important at this time.

They manifest a strong urge to share and take part in serious and fulfilling relationships and they have a heightened awareness of what is going on around them, perhaps greater than that of any other group.

<u>Group 4</u> people are more concerned with the larger picture and they can be dominant types who rule their space with assurance, but often also display a greater degree of flexibility and sensitivity.

They are particularly distinguished by an active imagination and fantasy life. The most successful of this mode can objectify those visions and perhaps make them a source of creativity rather than be victimized by them.

The allegiance of Group 4 is not so much to society or to personal considerations as to the world of ideas, where they are less concerned with the state of the world as it is now and more with how it could and should be.

Without making a meal of it, let us have a look at the personality traits of the first star sign, whereby:

The Aries is independent-minded, a thinker and a doer with little time for the established ways of doing things, unless they are personally tried and proven to fit a higher purpose, which cannot be explained or measured in real terms.

It needs to be in touch with reality, nevertheless, and so it has an extrovert and introvert nature, both of which are applied with an intensity reflecting the urgency of the knowledge needing to be discovered.

This can lead to an anxiety and nervousness whenever it is unable to act as desired or deemed necessary.

The esteem need may be predominant, leading to a vanity where the person may consider itself infallible and become absorbed by its intellect, whilst being driven by its curiosity over every idea, thought and happening in the world.

It must be absolutely occupied, where nothing is more horrible than an idle moment, as it throws itself into activities only to pass time.

Any profession that involves stirring up ideas, people and things whilst being the boss most of the time, is suitable for the first person in Group 1, as illustrated below under 'The Interaction Need Gratification'.

'The Higher Personalities' can be seen in our 'Desire + Ability + Opportunity = Behaviour to Suit' our cosmic connection and 'Our Ultimate Purpose in Life', as illustrated below "The Business of Creation".

The Business of Creation

Sign	Dates	Likes to:	Wants to know:
		Group 1 (Plan)	
1 Aries	(21/3 - 19/4)	Form a Hypothesis	What is the advantage to us?
2 Taurus	(20/4 - 20/5)	Test the Hypothesis	Who is the person in charge?
3 Gemini	(21/5 - 20/6)	Establish the Application	What are the obstacles?
		Group 2 (Prepare)	
4 Cancer	(21/6 - 22/7)	Build up a History	Has it been done before?
5 Leo	(23/7 - 22/8)	Develop a Technology	How does it work?
6 Virgo	(23/8 - 22/9)	Administer the System	What are the alternatives?
		Group 3 (Apply)	
7 Libra	(23/9 - 22/10)	Educate the Community	What are the likely problems?
8 Scorpio	(23/10 - 21/11)	Introduce into Community	How can we impress others?
9 Sagittarius	(22/11 - 21/12)	Measure the Benefits	How can we be accepted?
		Group 4 (Control)	
10 Capricorn	(22/12 - 19/1)	Maintain the Benefits	How much good does it do?
11 Aquarius	(20/1 - 18/2)	Review the Effectiveness	Whom does it good to?
12 Pisces	(19/2 - 20/3)	Discard the Technology	What are the actual benefits?

Fig.: 2.4.2

In that sense, Group 1 is focusing on the near future as it forms a hypothesis relating to a product/service, which is followed by Group 2 focusing on the present and the collection of data in order to build up a history

This is followed by Group 3 focusing on the recent past and Group 4 on the distant past as they contemplate their 'Need to Survive' here on earth within the prevailing environment of change and competition.

'The Higher Personalities' have appeared in a number of different ways over the years, one of which saw a similarity to the four seasons of Spring, (Plan) Summer, (Prepare) Autumn' (Apply) and Winter. (Control)

Another compared them to the predominant Action, Reason, Harmony and Excellence characteristics of Groups 1 to 4, respectively, whereas another saw a connection to the characteristics of:

The Performers—who are very good at using their five senses, which implies that they are spontaneous and tend to "live in the present", rather than plan and stick to a strict schedule.

They are usually creative and open-minded, love action and enjoy seeking new experiences.

The Intellectuals—who have strong intuitive and logical traits and put intellectual ability and reason above all else as they tend to be very analytical, inventive and inquisitive and shun emotions and sensual pleasures.

If you are arguing with an 'Intellectual', keep in mind that there is no point in appealing to their emotions—try presenting a logical counter-argument instead.

The Guardians—who have very strong principles and put security and stability first as they respect traditions, authority, law, follow rules or put them in place, especially when it comes to existing traditions and structures.

The 'Guardians' also see themselves as "model" citizens, which makes them excellent leaders, whilst their subordinates, colleagues or family members are likely to complain about their stubbornness and inflexibility.

The Idealists—who tend to be very idealistic, insightful and imaginative as they establish themselves as empathic visionaries, whose intuition helps them see patterns and links that may not be clear to other people.

The 'Idealists' strongly dislike conflict and criticism, but also share a very strong core of principles and ideas which usually means that people with these personality types are quite enigmatic and sensitive.

When we look at the different ways of presenting our 'Higher Personality', we will find a common denominator to our creative role and need to Plan, Prepare, Apply and Control 'The Business of Creation'.

The 'DISC' personality assessment and profiling system is frequently used by top management for understanding employees and building a better relationship with the management team and key employees.

In it there are four pure personality types:

1) 'D' which are <u>Dominate</u> or high drive, 2) 'I' which are <u>Influential</u> or highly social and great communicators, 3) 'S' which are <u>Steady</u> or very patient and thoughtful and 4) 'C' which are <u>Compliant</u> and want to get it right.

In that context, the 'D' and 'C' personality types are very 'task' orientated, whereas the 'I' and 'S' types are very 'relationship' orientated, which also identifies with the roles of modes (4), (3), (2) and (1) respectively.

This raises the question of 'Opportunity' relating to 'The Higher Personalities' and the powers of Mythology, the Military and to a lesser extent the Majority, who may want to suppress the personality traits as a matter of policy.

In other words, can the cosmic foetus be aborted by the political Parasites, Predators and, to a lesser extent, the Paradoxes of this world, or is 'The Survival of the Fairest' more powerful than 'The Survival of the Fittest'?

By all accounts, 'The Higher Personalities' cannot be suppressed forever, as their desire, ability and opportunity to advance the human race can also be applied to the destruction of an adverse political power.

And whilst this may involve the prolonged abuse or even sacrifice of the physical body as part of our commitment to the advancement of the human race, it has nevertheless taken the human race to where it is now.

At the same time, we still have a long way to go yet, like the powers of Morality and finally the powers of Mentality', the realization of which may be further illuminated by the 'The Psychology of Life' on earth.

2.5 The Psychology of Life

This brings us to the American professor of psychology Dr Clare W Graves wrote an article for 'The Futurist' magazine titled 'Human Nature Prepares for a Momentous Leap'.

In it, Graves described an impending change in human consciousness that would be:

'. . . the most difficult, but at the same time the most exciting transition the human race has faced to date, as it is not merely a transition to a new level of existence but the start of a new "movement" in the symphony of human history.'

Graves described human development as *'an unfolding, emergent, oscillating, spiralling process'* marked by progressive movement upwards through increasingly complex stages.

The process is like a pendulum that swings back and forth as we move upwards, which is ultimately an example of the dynamic balancing of opposites, (Yin and Yang) which we find in all natural systems.

The experience of growing from one stage to the next takes us from stability at the old stage through a journey into stress and chaos where the old stage structure falls apart, then on to reorganisation at a new and more complex stage.

We can notice there are two possible pathways shown, marked as individual stages and community stages, whereby the latter involves a breakthrough and a quantum leap, whilst the individual involves a much earlier response and consequently a smaller correction.

According to Graves, the most significant change ever seen in human consciousness occurs during the transition from Stage 6 to Stage 7, and by extension when a critical mass of people reach this transition our world will experience extraordinary change. Graves wasn't trying to predict the future, as he was simply observing human nature.

Stage 6—Preparing for the leap

Graves noted that Stages 1 to 6 were all focused on supporting oneself in the world and that they all inevitably caused excessive behaviours. The challenges that trigger the emergence of Stage 6 from the excesses of Stage 5, namely, materialism and overconsumption, burnout from too much time and effort spent pursuing individual performance goals, a growing social gap between the haves and have-nots, domination of the powerless, short sightedness and too much individualism resulting in a sense of loneliness and a lack of community.

Out of these perceived problems emerges Stage 6 behaviour, which attempts to bring things back into balance. Stage 6 behaviour is community focused and values personal feelings and social connections. It believes everything is relative and that there are many truths, not just one. Decision-making is by consensus, resources are shared and/or recycled and peace and harmony are highly valued.

During Stage 6, as well as focusing on the environment, community and social justice, there is also a strong desire to explore the inner workings of the human being, which leads to a great deal of introspection.

We are drawn to revisit all of our previous stages on an internal level and to heal past traumas that are stored within our body and psyche. One of the unfortunate side effects of this process is a greater tendency towards depression and self-harm.

A quick scan of the world in 2011 reveals an upsurge in Stage 6 behaviours, particularly in western countries. This is seen in the popularity of social media, growing community concern for the Earth's biosphere and resources, growing rejection of our Stage 5 dominated economic systems, and the rise of social movements actively protesting against and in some cases peacefully unseating governments that are operating from earlier stage thinking.

This evidence suggests we're moving rapidly towards a critical mass of people being at Stage 6. How many people constitute a critical mass is difficult to say, but with the aid of social media technology it's probably less than it used to be.

Stage 7—The leap

Graves wrote that the coping capacity or 'psychological space' of Stage 7 is greater than the sum of all the previous stages added together. This is a profound change that opens up a multidimensional awareness unlike anything that's come before. Stage 7 is the first of what Graves called the 'Being' levels, where our focus moves from a survival mindset to pondering the question: who am I being in the world?

The challenges that trigger the emergence of Stage 7 come from the excesses of Stage 6 plus the compounding excesses of Stages 3, 4 and 5, as many social problems begin to overlap on each other and multiplying the degree of challenge.

These include the depletion of natural resources, overpopulation, climate change and conflict and, while Stage 6 has good intentions, most of its attempted solutions are naïve and display an inability to comprehend complex adaptive systems, which in some cases actually make things worse.

Out of these perceived problems emerges Stage 7 behaviour, which is characterised by an absence of fear as a motivating factor and an absence of compulsiveness as Stage 7 moves beyond an objective, rational approach to a detached cognitive knowing; a trans-rational intuition.

With detachment comes the capacity to deal with problems without being swamped by them.

In an echo of the Stage 1 survival themes but at a global level, Stage 7 sees an urgent need for the restoration of our world so that life in all its forms, but especially humanity, can ensure long-term survival.

The Stage 7 approach is to consider the systemic whole, whilst working simultaneously across multiple dimensions, as it is highly adaptable and for the first time in human history has the conscious ability to swap and change between different behaviour sets.

If a problem emerges that requires a typical Stage 5 solution for example, then Stage 7 can adapt to operate like Stage 5.

A quick scan of the world today reveals growing evidence of Stage 7 behaviours, but because of its chameleon-like adaptability, it can be hard to see, unless we look for people who take a fearless approach, who are very accepting of others yet clear in their own mind as to what must be done; who avoid battling against archaic systems and governments, preferring instead to use minimal effort for maximum effect.

To paraphrase Buckminster Fuller, these are the people who'll build new systems that make the old systems obsolete. When Stage 7 reaches critical mass our world will change radically and quickly.

Stage 8—The neo-tribal revival

Stage 8 was the most advanced stage that Graves documented, although only six people out of the 1,065 people he studied (0.006%) showed evidence of it.

The primary challenge that triggers the emergence of Stage 8 is how to establish a new way of living that is in harmony with all human beings, other life forms and our planet's natural systems, and whilst Stage 7 sought to resolve the various crises that had arisen from the excesses of Stages 1-6, now our thinking turns to long-term stability.

We begin to see the Earth as one complex living system with its own intelligence and ourselves as an integral part of it all.

Stage 8 behaviour is characterised by, in Graves' own words, 'an almost mystical' nature which relies upon feelings and intuition much more than any previous stage. It embraces the mystery of existence and accepts that there are things we can never know; all we can really do is to simply be.

Just as Stage 7 has similarities with Stage 1 survivalism, Graves saw that Stage 8 is a much more sophisticated version of Stage 2 tribalism. Now the tribe is humanity itself and our sacred land is planet Earth.

There is a trend towards a non-interfering minimalistic lifestyle that is in harmony with nature, while maintaining all the advantages of our high technology. There's also an acceptance that the human tribe includes a wide variety of people spread across the many stages of development.

And so sustainable living means acknowledging, nurturing and guiding all these different peoples, their cultures, worldviews and their interaction with the planet and its resources.

Like Stage 7, Stage 8 can be difficult to see in the world due to its minimalistic approach and its chameleon-like adaptability. There is growing evidence though of a neo-tribal revival across the planet, including a growing interest in neo-shamanism and the use of psychoactive plants as allies in our own evolutionary process.

Our multilayered unfolding

Based on Dr Graves' research, the evidence suggests that we are indeed approaching a time of significant and rapid global change. Unlike some New Age predictions however, we're unlikely to see a sudden leap in consciousness that affects everyone at the same time.

Instead, history shows that human evolution is an emergent, oscillating, spiralling and unfolding process that ebbs and flows over time. As an example, the Stage 6 behaviour currently flaring up around the world was first noticed in the mid 1800s with the rise of civil rights movements in the USA. It likely inspired Einstein's theory of relativity and it played a prominent role in the counter-culture movement of the 1960s. It also powered the thinking behind the World Wide Web and the rise of environmental movements.

Stage 7 has also been around for a while, probably inspiring the birth of quantum science in the early 1900s, however, when a critical mass of people reach Stage 7, its global impact will be greater than any other change in human history.

In that context, we can expect to see significant changes to our ways of governing, our social systems and our technologies.

Again this is a gradual unfolding that's already underway, but current evidence suggests that we'll see the cultural equivalent of a record-breaking quantum leap in the not too distant future as altered state practices, rekindled by the neo-tribal pathfinders of Stage 8, may well play a significant role in accelerating this process.

It was also Dr. Clare Graves who inspired the idea for the 'Mauve Revolution', because of his focus on human consciousness as the locus of change and his pragmatic approach to what lay ahead.

According to David Scott; "The concept refers to a revolution in consciousness which is taking place before our very eyes, as we can see in the two-term election of Barak Obama, the Arab Spring, the election of Aung San Suu Kyi to the Burmese parliament, the granting of equal rights to Mother Nature in Ecuador, the legitimizing of third gender people in Nepal, the protest in Tiannamin Square, Gay people's right to marry, and so on.

Its essential features are equality, justice for all, a renewed affinity with nature, genuine participatory democracy and human rights, just to name a few.

It is a response to the previous age of materialism which has clearly overreached in its drive to create comfort and wealth and, while the age of materialism has produced a better life for many, as well as extraordinary advances in science and technology, it has also produced global warming, economic tyranny, gross exploitation of the masses by the few, and increasing alienation.

The new consciousness blossoming all over the planet is a watershed event in human history, as it represents a radical shift in worldview that was essentially unpredictable just a few decades ago.

Many thinkers have attempted to predict the impending cultural shift by placing it within a developmental model of human history like in the late Fifties, Teilhard de Chardin, the French philosopher-priest who foresaw the human race converging on an Omega Point of universal consciousness, and a couple of decades later, Alvin Toffler, who offered his vision of a Third Wave cresting in a post-industrial society."

Whilst Clare Graves passed away in 1986, a decade later two of his students, Don Beck and Christopher Cowan published their book, *Spiral Dynamics* which expanded on Graves' theory by substituting colours for the names of each level.

That is, Personalism became Green and Cognitive became Turquoise, whereby the colour choices were arbitrary and simply based on the authors' association of Green with the colour of "green politics, forests, and ecological consciousness," and Turquoise with "the colour of oceans and Earth as viewed from space."

And whilst the 'Mauve Revolution' developed from this idea, *Spiral Dynamics* posits a future not unlike that of Chardin in the form of a merging of personal and cosmic consciousness, whereby the "Self is part of a larger, conscious, spiritual whole that also serves self."

Unlike the authors of 'Spiral Dynamics' who felt that, if the universe began with a big bang, perhaps there was a consciousness that guided the pushing of the plunger that set it off, Graves said that at this level, "man will be driven by the winds of knowledge and human, and not godly, faith."

Others are of the view that the origins of the current revolution in consciousness are to be found in the Age of Enlightenment, in the 17th and 18th Century Europe which saw a dramatic rise in intellectual energy that questioned everything that had been accepted as gospel for more than a thousand years.

The attitude that awakened in the Enlightenment comprised challenges to moral values, traditions, religion, authority and even the motions of the planets.

The luminaries of this period include Spinoza, Locke, Voltaire, Rousseau, Montesquieu, Diderot, Leibniz, Newton, and Descartes, even though he came somewhat earlier.

In Descartes' fertile mind, the idea arose to see if he could reformulate philosophy from first principles, whereby his "method" was to place everything under the lens of his own doubt to see if something unassailable might remain.

Everything he considered withered in his sceptical evaluation, since he couldn't prove it wasn't all an illusion—with the one exception of his own mind as he couldn't doubt the very fact that he was doubting, which in itself was not an illusion.

"I think; therefore I am," he announced, which launched the phrase through the centuries which would have had a different flavour if he had said instead, "I doubt; therefore I am."

According to Robert Solomon, in his book, *Introducing Philosophy*, Descartes' method represented "one of the greatest revolutions in Western thought as, from Descartes on, the ultimate authority was to be found in man's own thinking and experience, and nowhere else."

Solomon summarized the essential principles of the Enlightenment as "the autonomy of the individual and each person's right to choose and to speak his own religious, political, moral, and philosophical beliefs, to 'pursue happiness' in his own way, and to lead the life that he, as a reasonable person, sees as right."

Of course, "the individual," at this time, meant white heterosexual male, whereby the expansion of the term to include women, other races, and gay people, would require another three hundred years.

A telling historical fact is that Britain didn't abolish slavery until 1834, (the United States not until 1865) which is another principle to consider is the pursuit of knowledge.

The Enlightenment was also the birth of modern science, as we can see in Galileo who overturned intuitive reason as the foundation for knowledge when, looking through his telescope, he saw that the earth actually revolved around the sun.

Needless to say, he was condemned by Church authorities for contradicting established wisdom insisting that the sun revolves around the earth.

In 1660, the Royal Society was formed in London as a gathering place for philosophers and scientists, where the spirit of the age may be summed up in the Society's motto: *Nullius in Verba*, or "Take nobody's word for it."

Knowledge now rested on experimental evidence as the scientific method became the established means of deciding what was true.

Commenting on the formation of the Royal Society, H.G. Wells observed, "The true scientific method is this: to make no unnecessary hypotheses, to trust no statements without verification, to test all things as rigorously as possible, to keep no secrets, to attempt no monopolies, to give out one's best modestly and plainly, serving no other end but knowledge."

From this point on, all truth statements had to respond to the question: Is it valid?

It would be extreme for us to suggest that the current culture wars are between pre and post Enlightenment like Fundamentalism vs. Pragmatism, Tyranny vs. Freedom, Favouritism vs. Egalitarianism, Folk Medicine vs. Science, Stigma vs. Inclusion and Chauvinism vs. Global Culture.

The principles of the Mauve Revolution may be summarized as follows:

Fairness, (freedom, equality, inclusion and dignity) Truth, (realism, scientific inquiry, and knowledge) Racial Equality, Gender Equality, Sexual Orientation Equality, People before Profits, (The Workplace) Planet before Profits, Justice, Children's rights, Animal Rights and

Realism (including the nature of Consciousness)

Source: 'The Mauve Revolution'—The Rationalist Approach to a New Global Consciousness.

On that note, let us reflect on the evolution of life on earth from the beginning of the cosmic egg to its fertilization and subsequent creation of a cosmic foetus, as illustrated below under "The Science of God".

The Science of God

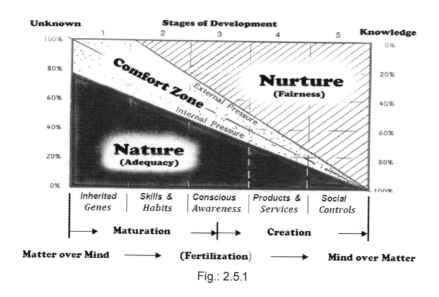

Fig.: 2.5.1

The illustration is portraying the 'Grand Order of Design' relating to the forces of Nature and 'The Survival of the Fittest' versus the forces of Nurture and 'The Survival of the Fairest'.

In that context, the great unknown manifested in our Nature has to be discovered during our Nurture by the prevailing businesses of industry and/or government representing the developing organs of a cosmic fetus.

In doing so, every person, product and power of social control is going through a cycle of life and death until the great unknown has been discovered and converted into a science relating to the 'Grand Order of Design'.

The motivation to do so is based on our desire to a) reduce the cost of living, and b) increase the quality of life in line with our conscious awareness of 'The Elements of Good & Evil' and 'Our Ultimate Purpose in Life'.

The entire process is based on internal pressures relating to the forces of Nature and adequacy of our basic needs, and external pressures relating to the forces of Nurture and fairness of our interaction needs.

The external pressures began with the emergence of the subconscious and its desire and ability to protect the life forms with the powers of hindsight relating to the life form from the time of its conception onwards.

This was followed by the emergence of the conscious, upon which the life forms were able to think for themselves with respect to the prevailing environment of change and competition and adapt their behaviour to suit.

Before long, the 'stable & predictable 'skills and habits were beginning to influence the growth and development of new life forms culminating in the emergence of archaic man and the maturation of the cosmic egg.

This was followed by the emergence of modern man representing the fertilization of the cosmic egg, upon which the human race began to multiply as if out of control, before differentiating in the realms of business.

In doing so, the businesses of industry and government had to compete with each other if they wanted to stay in business, which is somewhat different to our own growth and development in the womb.

But then again, our growth and development is based on our knowledge of the distant past and the recent past, whereas the growth of the cosmic fetus is based on 'our' knowledge of the near and distant future.

And so the growth and development of the cosmic fetus is taking its course as the businesses of industry and government are driving the needs and expectations of the community, and vice versa.

That is, the more the community had, the more it wanted, the reality of which can be seen in the gradual narrowing or tightening of its comfort zone until such time when it reaches a status of 'Mind over Matter'.

At that moment in time, we would not be alive in the traditional sense, as our notions and emotions are replaced by our 'stable & predictable' response to the 'universal' elements of change and competition.

In the meantime, we are caught up in a battle between the forces of Nature and Nurture as we are still heavily dependent on the natural resources and their conversion by the prevailing businesses of industry.

In doing so, we are more than willing to sacrifice our bodies and minds to the sciences of the day, as we are more than happy to throw caution to the wind with an optimistic outlook that defies all logic and reason.

For example, who in its right mind would be so stupid as to take up smoking, eating junk food, exposing their skin to the sun and risk skin cancer, dive head first into an unknown swimming hole, and so on, and so on.

As it happens, this is all part of 'The Human Condition' and 'Our Ultimate Purpose in Life', according to which "Many problems are caused by people, but they are also solved by people".

APPENDIX A

THE HISTORY OF "THE MEANING OF LIFE" SO FAR

Let us have a look at some of the earlier interpretations of the meaning of life or the significance of life or existence in general, which can also be expressed in different forms such as "Why are we here?", "What is life all about?" and "What is the purpose of our existence?"

The questions have been the subject of much philosophical, scientific, and theological speculation throughout history and there have been a large number of proposed answers to these questions from many different cultural and ideological backgrounds.

In the context of our inquiry, we will restrict our search for the meaning of life to western philosophical perspectives, beginning with Ancient Greek philosophy and:

Platonism—Plato was one of the earliest, most influential philosophers— mostly for idealism—a belief in the existence of universals. In the Theory of Forms, universals do not physically exist, like objects, but as heavenly forms.

In Platonism, the meaning of life is in attaining the highest form of knowledge, which is the Idea (Form) of the Good, from which all good and just things derive utility and value.

Aristotelianism—Aristotle, an apprentice of Plato, was another early and influential philosopher, who argued that ethical knowledge is not *certain* knowledge (such as metaphysics and epistemology), but is *general* knowledge.

Because it is not a theoretical discipline, a person had to study and practice in order to become "good"; thus if the person were to become virtuous, he could not simply study what virtue *is*, he had to *be* virtuous, via virtuous activities. To do this, Aristotle established what is virtuous, where:

Every skill and every inquiry, and similarly, every action and choice of action, is thought to have some good as its object. This is why the good has rightly been defined as the object of all endeavours, as everything is done with a goal, and that goal is "good".

Yet, if action A is done towards achieving goal B, then goal B also would have a goal, goal C, and goal C also would have a goal, and so would continue this pattern, until something stopped its infinite regression.

Aristotle's solution is the *Highest Good*, which is desirable for its own sake as is its own goal. The Highest Good is not desirable for the sake of achieving some other good, and all other "goods" desirable for its sake.

This involves achieving *eudemonia*, usually translated as "happiness", "well-being", "flourishing", and "excellence".

What is the highest good in all matters of action? To the name, there is almost complete agreement; for uneducated and educated alike call it happiness, and make happiness identical with the good life and successful living.

They disagree, however, about the meaning of happiness.

Cynicism—In the Hellenistic period, the Cynic philosophers said that the purpose of life is living a life of Virtue that agrees with Nature. Happiness depends upon being self-sufficient and master of one's mental attitude; suffering is the consequence of false judgments of value, which cause negative emotions and a concomitant vicious character.

The Cynical life rejects conventional desires for wealth, power, health, and fame, by being free of the possessions acquired in pursuing the conventional, and reasoning creatures or people could achieve happiness via rigorous training and by living in a way natural to human beings.

The world equally belongs to everyone, so suffering is caused by false judgments of what is valuable and what is worthless per the customs and conventions of society.

Cyrenaicism—founded by Aristippus of Cyrene, was an early Socratic school that emphasized only one side of Socrates' teachings—that happiness is one of the ends of moral action and that pleasure is the supreme good; thus a hedonistic world view, wherein bodily gratification is more intense than mental pleasure.

Cyrenaics prefer immediate gratification to the long-term gain of delayed gratification; denial is unpleasant unhappiness.

Epicureanism—To Epicurus, the greatest good is in seeking modest pleasures, to attain tranquility and freedom from fear via knowledge, friendship, and virtuous, temperate living; bodily pain is absent through one's knowledge of the workings of the world and of the limits of one's desires.

Combined, freedom from pain and freedom from fear are happiness in its highest form. Epicurus' lauded enjoyment of simple pleasures is quasi-ascetic "abstention" from sex and the appetites:

"When we say . . . that pleasure is the end and aim, we do not mean the pleasures of the prodigal or the pleasures of sensuality, as we are understood to do, by some, through ignorance, prejudice or wilful misrepresentation.

By pleasure we mean the absence of pain in the body and of trouble in the soul. It is not by an unbroken succession of drinking bouts and of revelry, not by sexual lust, nor the enjoyment of fish, and other delicacies of a luxurious table, which produce a pleasant life; it is sober reasoning, searching out the grounds of every choice and avoidance, and banishing those beliefs through which the greatest tumults take possession of the soul."

The Epicurean meaning of life rejects immortality and mysticism; there is a soul, but it is as mortal as the body. There is no afterlife, yet, one need not fear death, because "Death is nothing to us; for that which is dissolved, is without sensation, and that which lacks sensation is nothing to us."

Stoicism—teaches that living according to reason and virtue is to be in harmony with the universe's divine order, entailed by one's recognition of the universal *logos* (reason), an essential value of all people. The meaning of life is "freedom from suffering, passion and emotions", that is, being objective and having "clear judgement", *not* indifference.

Stoicism's prime directives are virtue, reason, and natural law, abided to develop personal self-control and mental fortitude as means of overcoming destructive emotions. The Stoic does not seek to extinguish emotions, only to avoid emotional troubles, by developing clear judgement and inner calm through diligently practiced logic, reflection, and concentration.

The Stoic ethical foundation is that "good lies in the state of the soul", itself, exemplified in wisdom and self-control, thus improving one's spiritual well-being: "*Virtue* consists in a *will* which is in agreement with Nature." The principle applies to one's personal relations thus: "to be free from anger, envy, and jealousy".

Enlightenment philosophy—Enlightenment and the colonial era both changed the nature of European philosophy and exported it worldwide. Devotion and subservience to God were largely replaced by notions of inalienable natural rights and the potentialities of reason, and universal ideals of love and compassion gave way to civic notions of freedom, equality, and citizenship.

The meaning of life changed as well, focusing less on humankind's relationship to God and more on the relationship between individuals and their society. This era is filled with theories that equate meaningful existence with the social order.

Classical liberalism—is a set of ideas that arose in the 17th and 18th centuries, out of conflicts between a growing, wealthy, propertied class and the established aristocratic and religious orders that dominated Europe.

Liberalism cast humans as beings with inalienable natural rights (including the right to retain the wealth generated by one's own work), and sought out means to balance rights across society. Broadly speaking, it considers individual liberty to be the most important goal, because only through ensured liberty are the other inherent rights protected.

There are many forms and derivations of liberalism, but their central conceptions of the meaning of life trace back to three main ideas.

Early thinkers such as John Locke, Jean-Jacques Rousseau and Adam Smith saw humankind beginning in the state of nature, then finding meaning for existence through labour and property, and using social contracts to create an environment that supports those efforts.

Kantianism—is a philosophy based on the ethical, epistemological, and metaphysical works of Immanuel Kant who is known for hisdeontological theory where there is a single moral obligation, the "Categorical Imperative", derived from the concept of duty and the view that the only intrinsically good thing is a good will; therefore an action can only be good if its maxim, the principle behind it, is duty to the moral law.

Kantians believe all actions are performed in accordance with some underlying maxim or principle, and for actions to be ethical, they must adhere to the categorical imperative.

Simply put, the test is that one must universalize the maxim (imagine that all people acted in this way) and then see if it would still be possible to perform the maxim in the world without contradiction.

In *Groundwork*, Kant gives the example of a person who seeks to borrow money without intending to pay it back. This is a contradiction because if it were a universal action, no person would lend money anymore as he knows that he will never be paid back. The maxim of this action, says Kant, results in a contradiction in conceivability (and thus contradicts perfect duty).

Kant also denied that the consequences of an act in any way contribute to the moral worth of that act, his reasoning being that the physical world is outside one's full control and thus one cannot be held accountable for the events that occur in it.

Utilitarianism—can be traced back as far as Epicurus, but, as a school of thought, it is credited to Jeremy Bentham, who found that "nature has placed mankind under the governance of two sovereign masters, pain and pleasure", then, from that moral insight, deriving the *Rule of Utility*: "that the good is whatever brings the greatest happiness to the greatest number of people". He defined the meaning of life as the "greatest happiness principle".

Jeremy Bentham's foremost proponent was James Mill, a significant philosopher in his day, and father of John Stuart Mill. The younger Mill was educated per Bentham's principles, including transcribing and summarizing much of his father's work.

Nihilism—suggests that life is without objective meaning. Friedrich Nietzsche characterized nihilism as emptying the world, and especially human existence, of meaning, purpose, comprehensible truth, and essential value; succinctly, nihilism is the process of "the devaluing of the highest values".

Seeing the nihilist as a natural result of the idea that God is dead, and insisting it was something to overcome, his questioning of the nihilist's life-negating values returned meaning to the Earth.

The End of the World—by John Martin.

To Martin Heidegger, nihilism is the movement whereby "being" is forgotten, and is transformed into value, in other words, the reduction of being to exchange value. Heidegger, in accordance with Nietzsche, saw in the so-called "death of God" a potential source for nihilism:

If God, as the supra-sensory ground and goal, of all reality, is dead; if the supra-sensory world of the Ideas has suffered the loss of its obligatory, and above it, its vitalizing and up-building power, then nothing more remains to which Man can cling, and by which he can orient himself.

The French philosopher Albert Camus asserts that the absurdity of the human condition is that people search for external values and meaning in a world which has none, and is indifferent to them.

Camus writes of value-nihilists such as Meursault, (a region in France that produces white wine from Chardonnay grapes), but also of values in a nihilistic world, that people can instead strive to be "heroic nihilists", living with dignity in the face of absurdity, living with "secular saintliness", fraternal solidarity, and rebelling against and transcending the world's indifference.

20th Century Philosophy—The current era has seen radical changes in both formal and popular conceptions of human nature, and the knowledge disclosed by modern science has effectively rewritten the relationship of humankind to the natural world.

Advances in medicine and technology have freed humans from significant limitations and ailments of previous eras; and philosophy—particularly following the linguistic turn—has altered how the relationships people have with themselves and each other are conceived.

Questions about the meaning of life have also seen radical changes, from attempts to re-evaluate human existence in biological and scientific terms (as in pragmatism and logical positivism) to efforts to meta-theorize about meaning-making as a personal, individual-driven activity (existentialism, secular humanism).

Pragmatism—originated in the late-19th-century U.S., to concern itself (mostly) with truth, positing that "only in struggling with the environment" do data, and derived theories, have meaning, and that *consequences*, like utility and practicality, are also components of truth.

Moreover, pragmatism posits that *anything* useful and practical is not always true, whilst arguing that what most contributes to the most human good in the long course is true. I

In practice, theoretical claims must be *practically verifiable*, i.e. one should be able to predict and test claims and that, ultimately, the needs of mankind should guide human intellectual inquiry.

Pragmatic philosophers suggest that the practical, useful understanding of life is more important than searching for an impractical abstract truth about life. William James argued that truth could be made, but not sought. To a pragmatist, the meaning of life is discoverable only via experience.

Theism—Theists believe God created the universe and that God had a purpose in doing so. Many theists, including the former atheist Anthony Flew, have been persuaded that God created because of the scientific evidence for a low entropy Big Bang more than 13 billion years ago.

Theists also hold the view that humans find their meaning and purpose for life in God's purpose in creating and further hold that if there were no God to give life ultimate meaning, value and purpose, then life would be absurd.

Existentialism—According to existentialism, each man and each woman creates the essence (meaning) of his and her life; life is not determined by a supernatural god or an earthly authority, one is free. As such, one's ethical prime directives are *action*, *freedom*, and *decision*, thus, existentialism opposes rationalism and positivism.

In seeking meaning to life, the existentialist looks to where people find meaning in life, in course of which using only reason as a source of meaning is insufficient; this gives rise to the emotions of anxiety and dread, felt in considering one's free will, and the concomitant awareness of death.

According to Jean-Paul Sartre, existence precedes essence; the (essence) of one's life arises *only* after one comes to existence.

Søren Kierkegaard spoke about a "leap", arguing that life is full of absurdity, and one must make his and her own values in an indifferent world. One can live meaningfully (free of despair and anxiety) in an unconditional commitment to something finite, and devotes that meaningful life to the commitment, despite the vulnerability inherent to doing so.[33]

Arthur Schopenhauer answered: "What is the meaning of life?" by stating that one's life reflects one's will, and that the will (life) is an aimless, irrational, and painful drive. Salvation, deliverance, and escape from suffering are in aesthetic contemplation, and sympathy for others.

For Friedrich Nietzsche, life is worth living only if there are goals inspiring one to live. Accordingly, he saw nihilism ("all that happens is meaningless") as without goals. He stated that asceticism denies one's living in the world; stated that values are not objective facts, that are rationally necessary, universally binding commitments: our evaluations are interpretations, and not reflections of the world, as it is, in itself, and, therefore, all ideations take place from a particular perspective.]

Absurdism—In absurdist philosophy, the Absurd arises out of the fundamental disharmony between the individual's search for meaning and the apparent meaninglessness of the universe. As beings looking for meaning in a meaningless world, humans have three ways of resolving the dilemma. Kierkegaard and Camus describe the solutions in their works, *The Sickness Unto Death* (1849) and *The Myth of Sisyphus* (1942):

Suicide (or, "escaping existence"): a solution in which a person simply ends one's own life. Both Kierkegaard and Camus dismiss the viability of this option.

Religious belief in a transcendent realm or being: a solution in which one believes in the existence of a reality that is beyond the Absurd, and, as such, has meaning. Kierkegaard stated that a belief in anything beyond the Absurd requires a non-rational but perhaps necessary religious acceptance in such an intangible and empirically unprovable thing (now commonly referred to as a "leap of faith"). However, Camus regarded this solution as "philosophical suicide".

Acceptance of the Absurd: a solution in which one accepts and even embraces the Absurd and continues to live in spite of it. Camus endorsed this solution, while Kierkegaard regarded this solution as "demoniac madness": "*He rages most of all at the thought that eternity might get it into its head to take his misery from him!*"

Secular Humanism—According to secular humanism, the human species came to be by reproducing successive generations in a progression of unguided evolution as an integral expression of nature, which is self-existing.

Human knowledge comes from human observation, experimentation, and rational analysis (the scientific method), and not from supernatural sources; the nature of the universe is what people discern it to be.

Likewise, "values and realities" are determined "by means of intelligent inquiry and "are derived from human need and interest as tested by experience", that is, by critical intelligence and, "As far as we know, the total personality is a function of the biological organism transacting in a social and cultural context."

People determine human purpose without supernatural influence; it is the human personality (general sense) that is the purpose of a human being's life. Humanism seeks to develop and fulfil, as "Humanism affirms our ability and responsibility to lead ethical lives of personal fulfilment that aspire to the greater good of humanity".

Humanism aims to promote enlightened self-interest and the common good for all people. It is based on the premises that the happiness of the individual person is inextricably linked to the well-being of all humanity, in part because humans are social animals who find meaning in personal relations and because cultural progress benefits everybody living in the culture.

The philosophical sub-genres of post-humanism and trans-humanism (sometimes used synonymously) are extensions of humanistic values. One should seek the advancement of humanity and of all life to the greatest degree feasible and seek to reconcile Renaissance humanism with the 21st century's techno scientific culture. In this light, every living creature has the right to determine its personal and social "meaning of life".

From a humanism-psychotherapeutic point of view, the question of the meaning of life could be reinterpreted as "What is the meaning of *my* life?"[43] This approach emphasizes that the question is personal—and avoids focusing on cosmic or religious questions about overarching purpose. There are many therapeutic responses to this question.

For example Viktor Frankl argues for "Dereflection", which translates largely as: cease endlessly reflecting on the self; instead, engage in life. On the whole, the therapeutic response is that the question itself—what is the meaning of life?—evaporates when one is fully engaged in life. (The question then morphs into more specific worries such as "What delusions am I under?"; "What is blocking my ability to enjoy things?"; "Why do I neglect loved-ones?")

Logical Positivism—Logical positivists ask: "What is the meaning of life?", "What is the meaning in asking?" and "If there are no objective values, then, is life meaningless?" Ludwig Wittgenstein and the logical positivists said: "Expressed in language, the question is meaningless"; because, *in* life the statement the "meaning of x", usually denotes the *consequences* of x, or the *significance* of x, or *what is notable* about x, etc., thus, when the meaning of life concept equals "x", in the statement the "meaning of x", the statement becomes recursive, and, therefore, nonsensical, or it might refer to the fact that biological life is essential to having a meaning in life.

The things (people, events) in the life of a person can have meaning (importance) as parts of a whole, but a discrete meaning of (the) life, itself, aside from those things, cannot be discerned.

A person's life has meaning (for himself, others) as the life events resulting from his achievements, legacy, family, etc., but, to say that life, itself, has meaning, is a misuse of language, since any note of significance, or of consequence, is relevant only *in* life (to the living), so rendering the statement erroneous.

Bertrand Russell wrote that although he found that his distaste for torture was not like his distaste for broccoli, he found no satisfactory, empirical method of proving this:

When we try to be definite, as to what we mean when we say that this or that is "the Good," we find ourselves involved in very great difficulties. Bentham's creed, that pleasure is the Good, roused furious opposition, and was said to be a pig's philosophy, and neither he nor his opponents could advance any argument.

In a scientific question, evidence can be adduced on both sides, and, in the end, one side is seen to have the better case—or, if this does not happen, the question is left undecided. But in a question, as to whether this, or that, is the ultimate Good, there is no evidence, either way; each disputant can only appeal to his own emotions, and employ such rhetorical devices as shall rouse similar emotions in others . . . Questions as to "values"—that is to say, as to what is good or bad on its own account, independently of its effects—lie outside the domain of science, as the defenders of religion emphatically assert.

I think that, in this, they are right, but, I draw the further conclusion, which they do not draw, that questions as to "values" lie wholly outside the domain of knowledge. That is to say, when we assert that this, or that, has "value", we are giving expression to our own emotions, not to a fact, which would still be true if our personal feelings were different.

Postmodernism—Postmodernist thought—broadly speaking—sees human nature as constructed by language, or by structures and institutions of human society. Unlike other forms of philosophy, postmodernism rarely seeks out *a priori* or innate meanings in human existence, but instead focuses on analyzing or critiquing *given* meanings in order to rationalize or reconstruct them.

Anything resembling a "meaning of life", in postmodernist terms, can only be understood within a social and linguistic framework, and must be pursued as an escape from the power structures that are already embedded in all forms of speech and interaction.

As a rule, postmodernists see awareness of the constraints of language as necessary to escaping those constraints, but different theorists take different views on the nature of this process: from radical reconstruction of meaning by individuals (as in deconstructionism) to theories in which individuals are primarily extensions of language and society, without real autonomy (as in post-structuralism).

In general, postmodernism seeks meaning by looking at the underlying structures that create or impose meaning, rather than the epiphenomenal appearances of the world.

Naturalistic Pantheism—According to naturalistic pantheism, the meaning of life is to care for and look after nature and the environment.

East Asian Philosophy—The Mohist philosophers believed that the purpose of life was universal, impartial love. Mohism promoted a philosophy of impartial caring—a person should care equally for all other individuals, regardless of their actual relationship.

The expression of this indiscriminate caring is what makes man a righteous being in Mohist thought. This advocacy of impartiality was a target of attack by the other Chinese philosophical schools, most notably the Confucians who believed that while love should be unconditional, it should not be indiscriminate. For example, children should hold a greater love for their parents than for random strangers.

Confucianism—recognizes human nature in accordance with the need for discipline and education. Because mankind is driven by both positive and negative influences, Confucianists see a goal in achieving virtue through strong relationships and reasoning as well as minimizing the negative. This emphasis on normal living is seen in the Confucianist scholar Tu Wei-Ming's quote, "we can realize the ultimate meaning of life in ordinary human existence."

Legalism (Chinese Philosophy)—The Legalists believed that finding the purpose of life was a meaningless effort. To the Legalists, only practical knowledge was valuable, especially as it related to the function and performance of the state.

Religious perspectives—The religious perspectives on the meaning of life are those ideologies which explain life in terms of an implicit purpose not defined by humans.

<u>Western Religions</u>—Christianity has its roots in Judaism, and shares much of the latter faith's ontology, its central beliefs derive from the teachings of Jesus Christ, as presented in the New Testament. Life's purpose in Christianity is to seek divine salvation through the grace of God and intercession of Christ.

The New Testament speaks of God wanting to have a relationship with humans both in this life and the life to come, which can happen only if one's sins are forgiven(John 3:16-21; 2 Peter 3:9).

In the Christian view, humankind was made in the Image of God and perfect, but the Fall of Man caused the progeny of the first Parents to inherit Original Sin. The sacrifice of Christ's passion, death and resurrection provide the means for transcending that impure state (Romans 6:23).

The means for doing so varies between different groups of Christians, but all rely on belief in Jesus, his work on the cross and his resurrection as the fundamental starting point for a relationship with God. Faith in God is found in Ephesians 2:8-9—"For by grace you have been saved through faith; and that not of yourselves, it is the gift of God; not as a result of works, that no one should boast." (New American Standard Bible, 1973).

A recent alternative Christian theological discourse interprets Jesus as revealing that the purpose of life is to elevate our compassionate response to human suffering.

Nonetheless the conventional Christian position is that people are justified by belief in the propitiatory sacrifice of Jesus' death on the cross. The Gospel maintains that through this belief, the barrier that sin has created between man and God is destroyed, and allows God to change people and instil in them a new heart after his own will, and the ability to do it. This is what the terms "reborn" or "saved" almost always refer to.

In the *Westminster Shorter Catechism*, the first question is: "What is the chief end of Man?", that is, "What is Man's main purpose?" The answer is:

"Man's chief end is to glorify God, and enjoy him forever". God requires one to obey the revealed moral law saying: "love the Lord your God with all your heart, with all your soul, with all your strength, and with all your mind; and your neighbour as yourself".

The *Baltimore Catechism* answers the question "Why did God make you?" by saying "God made me to know Him, to love Him, and to serve Him in this world, and to be happy with Him forever in heaven."

The Apostle Paul also answers this question in his speech on the Areopagus in Athens: "And He has made from one blood every nation of men to dwell on all the face of the earth, and has determined their pre-appointed times and the boundaries of their dwellings, so that they should seek the Lord, in the hope that they might grope for Him and find Him, though He is not far from each one of us."

According to Revelation 4:11; everything exists for God's pleasure.

The Church of Jesus Christ of Latter Day Saints (Mormons) teaches that the purpose of life on Earth is to gain knowledge and experience. Mormons believe that God the Father first created humans as spirits, each with the potential to progress toward perfection. Earth life is considered a crucial stage in this development—wherein a physical body, coupled with the freedom to choose, makes for an ideal environment to learn and grow.

The Fall of Adam is not viewed as a "change of plans", rather it was a necessary step because only through the opposition found in mortality can mankind learn the difference between good and evil (Genesis 3:22, 2 Nephi 2:11[56]). God provides instruction to mortals on how to choose good over evil by revealing it through chosen prophets.

This instruction includes the concept of repentance as a lifelong growth process through which mankind continuously learns to make better choices by forsaking sin and learning from mistakes. Throughout this process, baptized members can regularly invoke the cleansing power of Christ's atonement through the weekly ordinance of the sacrament (Luke 22:17-20).

It is by this cleansing power of the atonement that mortals are made worthy to return to the presence of the Father, where they can continue to build upon the wisdom gained during mortality (Doctrine and Covenants 130:18-19[57]) and ultimately fulfil their end purpose, which is to attain a fullness of joy by inheriting God's glory (Romans 8:16-17, Galatians 4:7)—in other words, his intelligence (Doctrine and Covenants 93:36; 50:24).

Islam—In Islam, man's ultimate life objective is to worship the creator Allah (God) by abiding by the Divine guidelines revealed in the Qur'an and the Tradition of the Prophet. Earthly life is merely a test, determining one's afterlife, either in *Jannah* (Paradise) or in *Jahannam* (Hell).

For Allah's satisfaction, via the Qur'an, all Muslims must believe in God, his revelations, his angels, his messengers, and in the "Day of Judgment". The Qur'an describes the purpose of creation as follows: "Blessed be he in whose hand is the kingdom, he is powerful over all things, who created death and life that he might examine which of you is best in deeds, and he is the almighty, the forgiving" (Qur'an 67:1-2) and "And I (Allah) created not the jinn and mankind except that they should be obedient (to Allah)." (Qur'an 51:56).

Obedience testifies to the oneness of God in his lordship, his names, and his attributes. Terrenal life is a test; how one *acts* (behaves) determines whether one's soul goes to Jannat (Heaven) or to Jahannam (Hell) However on the day of Judgement the final decision is of Allah alone. Allah may cover up short comings and allow some people to go to heaven even though they may have some sins in the record.

The Five Pillars of Islam are duties incumbent to every Muslim; they are: Shahadah (profession of faith); Salah (ritual prayer); Zakah (charity); Sawm (fasting during Ramadan), and Hajj (pilgrimage to Mecca). They derive from the Hadith works, notably of Sahih Al-Bukhari and Sahih Muslim. The five pillars are not mentioned directly in the Quran.

Beliefs differ among the Kalam. The Sunni concept of pre-destination is divine decree; likewise, the Shi'a concept of pre-destination is divine justice; in the esoteric view of the Sufis, the universe exists only for God's pleasure; Creation is a grand game, wherein Allah is the greatest prize.

The Sufi view of the meaning of life stems from the hadith qudsi that states "I (God) was a Hidden Treasure and loved to be known. Therefore I created the Creation that I might be known." One possible interpretation of this view is that the meaning of life for an individual is to know the nature of God, and the purpose of all of creation is to reveal that nature, and to prove its value as the ultimate treasure, that is God. However, this hadith is stated in various forms and interpreted in various ways by people, such, as 'Abdu'l-Bahá of the Bahá'í Faith,[63] and in Ibn'Arabī's Fuṣūṣ al-Ḥikam.

Bahá'í Faith—The Bahá'í Faith emphasizes the unity of humanity. To Bahá'ís, the purpose of life is focused on spiritual growth and service to humanity. Human beings are viewed as intrinsically spiritual beings. People's lives in this material world provide extended opportunities to grow, to develop divine qualities and virtues, and the prophets were sent by God to facilitate this.

Judaism—In the Judaic world view, the meaning of life is to elevate the physical world ('Olam HaZeh') and prepare it for the world to come ('Olam HaBa'), the messianic era. This is called Tikkun Olam ("Fixing the World"). Olam HaBa can also mean the spiritual afterlife, and there is debate concerning the eschatological order. However, Judaism is not focused on personal salvation, but on communal (between man and man) and individual (between man and God) spiritualized actions in this world.

Judaism's most important feature is the worship of a single, incomprehensible, transcendent, one, indivisible, absolute Being, who created and governs the universe. Closeness with the God of Israel is through study of His Torah, and adherence to its mitzvot (divine laws).

In traditional Judaism, God established a special covenant with a people, the people of Israel, at Mount Sinai, giving the Jewish commandments. Torah comprises the written Pentateuch and the transcribed oral tradition, further developed through the generations.

The Jewish people are intended as "a kingdom of priests and a holy nation"[68] and a "light to the Nations", influencing the other peoples to keep their own religio-ethical Seven Laws of Noah. The messianic era is seen as the perfection of this dual path to God.

Jewish observances involve ethical and ritual, affirmative and prohibitive injunctions. Modern Jewish denominations differ over the nature, relevance and emphases of mitzvot. Jewish philosophy emphasises that God is not affected or benefited, but the individual and society benefit by drawing close to God.

The rationalist Maimonides sees the ethical and ritual divine commandments as a necessary, but insufficient preparation for philosophical understanding of God, with its love and awe. Among fundamental values in the Torah are pursuit of justice, compassion, peace, kindness, hard work, prosperity, humility, and education. The world to come, prepared in the present, elevates man to an everlasting connection with God.

Simeon the Righteous says, "the world stands on three things: on Torah, on worship, and on acts of loving kindness." The prayer book relates, "blessed is our God who created us for his honour . . . and planted within us everlasting life." Of this context, the Talmud states, "everything that God does is for the good," including suffering.

The Jewish mystical Kabbalah gives complimentary esoteric meanings of life. As well as Judaism providing an immanent relationship with God (personal theism), in Kabbalah the spiritual and physical creation is a paradoxical

201

manifestation of the immanent aspects of God's Being (panentheism), related to the Shekhinah (Divine feminine). Jewish observance unites the sephirot (Divine attributes) on high, restoring harmony to creation.

In Lurianic Kabbalah, the meaning of life is the messianic rectification of the shattered sparks of God's persona, exiled in physical existence (the Kelipot shells), through the actions of Jewish observance.] Through this, in Hasidic Judaism the ultimate essential "desire" of God is the revelation of the Omnipresent Divine essence through materiality, achieved by man from within his limited physical realm, when the body will give life to the soul.

Zoroastrianism—is the religion and philosophy named after its prophet Zoroaster, which is believed to have influenced the beliefs of Judaism and its descendant religions.[76]Zoroastrians believe in a universe created by a transcendental God, Ahura Mazda, to whom all worship is ultimately directed. Ahura Mazda's creation is *asha*, truth and order, and it is in conflict with its antithesis, *druj*, falsehood and disorder.

Since humanity possesses free will, people must be responsible for their moral choices. By using free will, people must take an active role in the universal conflict, with good thoughts, good words and good deeds to ensure happiness and to keep chaos at bay.

South Asian religions—Hindu philosophies—Hinduism is a religious category including many beliefs and traditions. Since Hinduism was the way of expressing meaningful living for a long time, before there was a need for naming it as a separate religion, Hindu doctrines are supplementary and complementary in nature, generally non-exclusive, suggestive and tolerant in content.

Most believe that the ātman (spirit, soul)—the person's true *self*—is eternal. In part, this stems from Hindu beliefs that spiritual development occurs across many lifetimes, and goals should match the state of development of the individual.

There are four possible aims to human life, known as the *purusharthas* (ordered from least to greatest): *Kāma* (wish, desire, love and sensual pleasure), *Artha* (wealth, prosperity, glory), *Dharma* (righteousness, duty, morality, virtue, ethics), encompassing notions such as *ahimsa* (non-violence) and satya (truth) and *Moksha* (liberation, i.e. liberation from the cycle of reincarnation).

In all schools of Hinduism, the meaning of life is tied up in the concepts of karma (causal action), sansara (the cycle of birth and rebirth), and moksha (liberation). Existence is conceived as the progression of the ātman (similar to the western concept of a soul) across numerous lifetimes, and its ultimate progression towards liberation from karma.

Particular goals for life are generally subsumed under broader yogas (practices) or dharma (correct living) which is intended to create more favourable reincarnations, though they are generally positive acts in this life as well.

Traditional schools of Hinduism often worship Devas which are manifestations of Ishvara (a personal or chosen God); these Devas are taken as ideal forms to be identified with, as a form of spiritual improvement.

In short, the goal is to realize the fundamental truth about oneself. This thought is conveyed in the Mahāvākyas ("Tat Tvam Asi" (thou art that), "Aham Brahmāsmi", "Prajñānam Brahma" and "Ayam Ātmā Brahma" (the soul and the world are one)).

Advaita and Dvaita Hinduism—Later schools reinterpreted the vedas to focus on Brahman, "The One Without a Second", as a central God-like figure.

In monist Advaita Vedanta, ātman is ultimately indistinguishable from Brahman, and the goal of life is to know or realize that one's ātman (soul) is identical to Brahman. To the Upanishads, whoever becomes fully aware of the ātman, as one's core of self, realizes identity with Brahman, and, thereby, achieves Moksha (liberation, freedom).

Dualist Dvaita Vedanta and other bhakti schools have a dualist interpretation. Brahman is seen as a supreme being with a personality and manifest qualities. The ātman depends upon Brahman for its existence; the meaning of life is achieving Moksha through love of God and upon His grace.

Vaishnavism—is a branch of Hinduism in which the principal belief is the identification of Vishnu or Narayana as the one supreme God. This belief contrasts with the Krishna-centred traditions, such as Vallabha, Nimbaraka and Gaudiya, in which Krishna is considered to be the One and only Supreme God and the source of all avataras.

Vaishnava theology includes the central beliefs of Hinduism such as monotheism, reincarnation, samsara, karma, and the various Yoga systems, but with a particular emphasis on devotion (bhakti) to Vishnu through the process of Bhakti yoga, often including singing Vishnu's name's (bhajan), meditating upon his form (dharana) and performing deity worship (puja). The practices of deity worship are primarily based on texts such as Pañcaratra and various Samhitas.

One popular school of thought, Gaudiya Vaishnavism, teaches the concept of Achintya Bheda Abheda. In this, Krishna is worshipped as the single true God, and all living entities are eternal parts and the Supreme Personality of the Godhead Krishna. Thus the constitutional position of a living entity is to serve the Lord with love and devotion. The purpose of human life especially is to think beyond the animalistic way of eating, sleeping, mating and defending and engage the higher intelligence to revive the lost relationship with Krishna.

Jainism—is a religion originating in ancient India, its ethical system promotes self-discipline above all else.

Through following the ascetic teachings of Jina, a human achieves enlightenment (perfect knowledge). Jainism divides the universe into living and non-living beings. Only when the living become attached to the non-living does suffering result. Therefore, happiness is the result of self-conquest and freedom from external objects. The meaning of life may then be said to be to use the physical body to achieve self-realization and bliss.[1]

Jains believe that every human is responsible for his or her actions and all living beings have an eternal soul, *jiva*. Jains believe all souls are equal because they all possess the potential of being liberated and attaining Moksha. The Jain view of karma is that every action, every word, every thought produces, besides its visible, an invisible, transcendental effect on the soul.

Jainism includes strict adherence to ahimsa (or *ahinsā*), a form of nonviolence that goes far beyond vegetarianism. Jains refuse food obtained with unnecessary cruelty. Many practice a lifestyle similar to veganism due to the violence of modern dairy farms, and others exclude root vegetables from their diets in order to preserve the lives of the plants from which they eat.

Buddhism—Buddhists practice to embrace with mindfulness the ill-being (suffering) and well-being that is present in life. Buddhists practice to see the causes of ill-being and well-being in life. For example, one of the causes of suffering is unhealthy attachment to objects material or non-material. The Buddhist sūtras and tantras do not speak about "the meaning of life" or "the purpose of life", but about the potential of human life to end suffering, for example through embracing (not suppressing or denying) cravings and conceptual attachments. Attaining and perfecting dispassion is a process of many levels that ultimately results in the state of Nirvana. Nirvana means freedom from both suffering and rebirth.

Theravada Buddhism is generally considered to be close to the early Buddhist practice. It promotes the concept of Vibhajjavada (Pali), literally "Teaching of Analysis", which says that insight must come from the aspirant's experience, critical investigation, and reasoning instead of by blind faith.

However, the Theravadin tradition also emphasizes heeding the advice of the wise, considering such advice and evaluation of one's own experiences to be the two tests by which practices should be judged. The Theravadin goal is liberation (or freedom) from suffering, according to the Four Noble Truths. This is attained in the achievement of Nirvana, or Unbinding which also ends the repeated cycle of birth, old age, sickness and death.

Mahayana Buddhism—Mahayana Buddhist schools de-emphasize the traditional view (still practiced in Theravada) of the release from individual Suffering (Dukkha) and attainment of Awakening (Nirvana). In Mahayana, the Buddha is seen as an eternal, immutable, inconceivable, omnipresent being.

The fundamental principles of Mahayana doctrine are based on the possibility of universal liberation from suffering for all beings, and the existence of the transcendent Buddha-nature, which is the eternal Buddha essence present, but hidden and unrecognized, in all living beings.

Philosophical schools of Mahayana Buddhism, such as Chan/Zen and the vajrayana Tibetan and Shingon schools, explicitly teach that bodhisattvas should refrain from full liberation, allowing themselves to be reincarnated into the world until all beings achieve enlightenment. Devotional schools such as Pure Land Buddhism seek the aid of celestial buddhas—individuals who have spent lifetimes accumulating positive karma, and use that accumulation to aid all.

Sikhism—The monotheistic Sikh religion was founded by Guru Nanak Dev, the term "sikh" means student, which denotes that followers will lead their lives forever learning. This system of religious philosophy and expression has been traditionally known as the Gurmat (literally "the counsel of the gurus") or the Sikh Dharma.

The followers of Sikhism are ordained to follow the teachings of the ten Sikh Gurus, or enlightened leaders, as well as the holy scripture entitled the *Gurū Granth Sāhib*, which includes selected works of many philosophers from diverse socio-economic and religious backgrounds.

The Sikh Gurus say that salvation can be obtained by following various spiritual paths, so Sikhs do not have a monopoly on salvation: "The Lord dwells in every heart, and every heart has its own way to reach Him." Sikhs believe that all people are equally important before God. Sikhs balance their moral and spiritual values with the quest for knowledge, and they aim to promote a life of peace and equality but also of positive action.

A key distinctive feature of Sikhism is a non-anthropomorphic concept of God, to the extent that one can interpret God as the Universe itself (pantheism). Sikhism thus sees life as an opportunity to understand this God as well as to discover the divinity which lies in each individual.

While a full understanding of God is beyond human beings, Nanak described God as not wholly unknowable, and stressed that God must be seen from "the inward eye", or the "heart", of a human being: devotees must meditate to progress towards enlightenment and the ultimate destination of a Sikh is to lose the ego completely in the love of the lord and finally merge into the almighty creator.

Nanak emphasized the revelation through meditation, as its rigorous application permits the existence of communication between God and human beings.

East Asian religions, Taoism—symbolizes the unity of opposites between yin and yang.

Taoist cosmogony emphasizes the need for all sentient beings and all man to return to the *primordial* or to rejoin with the *Oneness* of the Universe by way of self-cultivation and self-realization. All adherents should understand and be in tune with the ultimate truth.

Taoists believe all things were originally from Taiji and Tao, and the meaning in life for the adherents is to realize the temporal nature of the existence. "Only introspection can then help us to find our innermost reasons for living . . . the simple answer is here within ourselves."

Shinto—is the native religion of Japan. Shinto means "the path of the kami", but more specifically, it can be taken to mean "the divine crossroad where the kami chooses his way". The "divine" crossroad signifies that all the universe is divine spirit. This foundation of free will, choosing one's way, means that life is a creative process.

Shinto wants life to live, not to die. Shinto sees death as pollution and regards life as the realm where the divine spirit seeks to purify itself by rightful self-development. Shinto wants individual human life to be prolonged forever on earth as a victory of the divine spirit in preserving its objective personality in its highest forms.

The presence of evil in the world, as conceived by Shinto, does not stultify the divine nature by imposing on divinity responsibility for being able to relieve human suffering while refusing to do so. The sufferings of life are the sufferings of the divine spirit in search of progress in the objective world.[96]

New Religions—There are many new religious movements in East Asia, and some with millions of followers: Chondogyo, Tenrikyo, Cao Đài, and Seicho-No-Ie. New religions typically have unique explanations for the meaning of life. For example, in Tenrikyo, one is expected to live a Joyous Life by participating in practices that create happiness for oneself and others.

Scientific Inquiry and Perspectives—Members of the scientific community and philosophy of science communities believe that science may be able to provide some context, and set some parameters for conversations on topics related to meaning in life. This includes offering insights from the science of happiness or studies of death anxiety. This also means providing context for, and understanding of life itself through explorations of the Big Bang, the origin of life, and evolution.

Psychological significance and value in life—Science may or may not be able to tell us what is of essential value in life (and various materialist philosophies such as dialectical materialism challenge the very idea of an absolute value or meaning of life), but some studies definitely bear on aspects of the question: researchers in positive psychology (and, earlier and less rigorously, in humanistic psychology) study factors that lead to life satisfaction, full engagement in activities, making a fuller contribution by utilizing one's personal strengths, and meaning based on investing in something larger than the self.

One value system suggested by social psychologists, broadly called Terror Management Theory, states that human meaning is derived from a fundamental fear of death, and values are selected when they allow us to escape the mental reminder of death.

Neuroscience describes reward, pleasure, and motivation in terms of neurotransmitter activity, especially in the limbic system and the ventral tegmental area in particular. If one believes that the meaning of life is to maximize pleasure and to ease general life, then this allows normative predictions about how to act to achieve this. Likewise, some ethical naturalists advocate a science of morality—the empirical pursuit of flourishing for all conscious creatures.

Sociology examines value at a social level using theoretical constructs such as value theory, norms, anomie, etc.

Origin and nature of biological life—The exact mechanisms of abiogenesis are unknown: notable hypotheses include the RNA world hypothesis (RNA-based replicators) and the iron-sulfur world theory (metabolism without genetics). The process by which different life forms have developed throughout history via genetic mutation and natural selection is explained by evolution.

At the end of the 20th century, based upon insight gleaned from the gene-centred view of evolution, biologists George C. Williams, Richard Dawkins, David Haig, among others, concluded that if there is a primary function to life, it is the replication of DNA and the survival of one's genes.

This view has not achieved universal agreement; Jeremy Griffith is a notable exception, maintaining that the meaning of life is to be integrative.

Though scientists have intensively studied life on Earth, defining life in unequivocal terms is still a challenge. Physically, one may say that life "feeds on negative entropy" which refers to the process by which living entities decrease their internal entropy at the expense of some form of energy taken in from the environment.

Biologists generally agree that life forms are self-organizing systems regulating the internal environment as to maintain this organized state, metabolism serves to provide energy, and reproduction causes life to continue over a span of multiple generations. Typically, organisms are responsive to stimuli and genetic information changes from generation to generation, resulting in adaptation through evolution; this optimizes the chances of survival for the individual organism and its descendants respectively.

Non-cellular replicating agents, notably viruses, are generally not considered to be organisms because they are incapable of independent reproduction or metabolism. This classification is problematic, though, since some parasites and endosymbionts are also incapable of independent life. Astrobiology studies the possibility of different forms of life on other worlds, including replicating structures made from materials other than DNA.

Origins and ultimate fate of the universe—The metric expansion of space. The inflationary epoch is the expansion of the metric tensor at left.

Though the Big Bang theory was met with much scepticism when first introduced, it has become well-supported by several independent observations. However, current physics can only describe the early universe from 10^{-43} seconds after the Big Bang (where zero time corresponds to infinite temperature); a theory of quantum gravity would be required to understand events before that time.

Nevertheless, many physicists have speculated about what would have preceded this limit, and how the universe came into being. For example, one interpretation is that the Big Bang occurred coincidentally, and when considering the anthropic principle, it is sometimes interpreted as implying the existence of a multiverse.

The ultimate fate of the universe, and implicitly humanity, is hypothesized as one in which biological life will eventually become unsustainable, such as through a Big Freeze, Big Rip, or Big Crunch.

Scientific questions about the mind—The nature and origin of consciousness and the mind itself are also widely debated in science. The explanatory gap is generally equated with the hard problem of consciousness, and the question of free will is also considered to be of fundamental importance.

These subjects are mostly addressed in the fields of cognitive science, neuroscience (e.g. the neuroscience of free will) and philosophy of mind, though some evolutionary biologists and theoretical physicists have also made several allusions to the subject.

Reductionist and eliminative materialistic approaches, for example the Multiple Drafts Model, hold that consciousness can be wholly explained by neuroscience through the workings of the brain and its neurons, thus adhering to biological naturalism.[116][117][118]

On the other hand, some scientists, like Andrei Linde, have considered that consciousness, like spacetime, might have its own intrinsic degrees of freedom, and that one's perceptions may be as real as (or even more real than) material objects. Hypotheses of consciousness and spacetime explain consciousness in describing a "space of conscious elements", often encompassing a number of extra dimensions.

Electromagnetic theories of consciousness solve the binding problem of consciousness in saying that the electromagnetic field generated by the brain is the actual carrier of conscious experience, there is however disagreement about the implementations of such a theory relating to other workings of the mind.

Quantum mind theories use quantum theory in explaining certain properties of the mind. Explaining the process of free will through quantum phenomena is a popular alternative to determinism, such postulations may variously relate free will to quantum fluctuations, quantum amplification, quantum potential and quantum probability.

Based on the premises of non-materialistic explanations of the mind, some have suggested the existence of a cosmic consciousness, asserting that consciousness is actually the "ground of all being". Proponents of this view cite accounts of paranormal phenomena, primarily extrasensory perceptions and psychic powers, as evidence for an incorporeal higher consciousness.

In hopes of proving the existence of these phenomena, parapsychologists have orchestrated various experiments, but apparently successful results are more likely due to sloppy procedures, poorly trained researchers, or methodological flaws than to actual effects.

Physical Health—Emerging research shows that meaning in life predicts better physical health outcomes. Greater meaning has been associated with a reduced risk of Alzheimer's disease, reduced risk of heart attack among individuals with coronary heart disease, reduced risk of stroke, and increased longevity in both American and Japanese samples.

The mystery of life and its meaning is an often recurring subject in popular culture, featured in entertainment media and various forms of art.

In Douglas Adams' popular comedy book, movie, television, and radio series *The Hitchhiker's Guide to the Galaxy*, the Answer to the Ultimate Question of Life, the Universe, and Everything is given the numeric solution "42", after seven and a half million years of calculation by a giant supercomputer called Deep Thought.

When this answer is met with confusion and anger from its constructors, Deep Thought explains that "I think the problem, to be quite honest with you, is that you've never actually known what the question is."

In the continuation of the book, the question is proposed to be the song of Bob Dylan "How many roads must a man walk down, before you can call him a man." In the sequel, *The Restaurant at the End of the Universe*, it states that the question is 6x9. While 6 x 9 = 54 in base 10, it does equal 42 in base 13, which author Adams claimed was completely serendipitous.

In *Monty Python's 'The Meaning of Life'*,—there are several allusions to the meaning of life. At the end of the film, a character played by Michael Palin is handed an envelope containing "the meaning of life", which he opens and reads out to the audience: "Well, it's nothing very special. Uh, try to be nice to people, avoid eating fat, read a good book every now and then, get some walking in, and try to live together in peace and harmony with people of all creeds and nations."

Many other Python sketches and songs are also existential in nature, questioning the importance we place on life ("Always Look on the Bright Side of Life") and other meaning-of-life related questioning. John Cleese also had his sit-com character Basil Fawlty contemplating the futility of his own existence in Fawlty Towers.

In *The Simpsons* episode "Homer the Heretic", a representation of God agrees to tell Homer what the meaning of life is, but the show's credits begin to roll just as he starts to say what it is.

Popular views—"What is the meaning of life?" is a question many people ask themselves at some point during their lives, most in the context "What is the purpose of life?" Some popular answers include:

To realize one's potential and ideals:

- To chase dreams.
- To live one's dreams.
- To spend it for something that will outlast it.
- To matter, to count, stand for something, or have made some difference by having lived.
- To expand one's potential in life.
- To become the person you've always wanted to be.
- To become the best version of yourself.
- To seek happiness and flourish.
- To be a true authentic human being.
- To be able to put the whole of oneself into one's feelings, one's work, one's beliefs.[144]
- To follow or submit to our destiny.
- To achieve eudaimonia, a flourishing of human spirit.

To achieve biological perfection:

- To survive, that is, to live as long as possible, including pursuit of immortality (through scientific means).
- To live forever or die trying.
- To evolve.
- To replicate, to reproduce. "The 'dream' of every cell is to become two cells."

To seek wisdom and knowledge:

- To expand one's perception of the world.
- To follow the clues and walk out the exit.
- To learn as many things as possible in life.

- To know as much as possible about as many things as possible.
- To seek wisdom and knowledge and to tame the mind, as to avoid suffering caused by ignorance and find happiness.
- To face our fears and accept the lessons life offers us.
- To find the meaning or purpose of life.
- To find a reason to live.
- To resolve the imbalance of the mind by understanding the nature of reality.

To do good, to do the right thing:

- To leave the world as a better place than you found it.
- To do your best to leave every situation better than you found it.
- To benefit others.
- To give more than you take.
- To end suffering.
- To create equality.
- To challenge oppression.
- To distribute wealth.
- To be generous.
- To contribute to the well-being and spirit of others.
- To help others, to help one another.
- To take every chance to help another while on your journey here.
- To be creative and innovative.
- To forgive.
- To accept and forgive human flaws.
- To be emotionally sincere.
- To be responsible.
- To be honourable.
- To seek peace.

Meanings relating to religion:

- To reach the highest heaven and be at the heart of the Divine.
- To have a pure soul and experience God.

215

- To understand the mystery of God.
- To know or attain union with God.
- To know oneself, know others, and know the will of heaven.
- To love something bigger, greater, and beyond ourselves, something we did not create or have the power to create, something intangible and made holy by our very belief in it.
- To love God and all of his creations.
- To glorify God by enjoying him forever.
- To go and make new disciples of Jesus Christ.
- To act justly, love mercy, and walk humbly with your God.
- To be fruitful and multiply. (Genesis 1:28)
- To obtain freedom (Romans 8:20-21)
- To fill the Earth and subdue it. (Genesis 1:28)

To love, to feel, to enjoy the act of living:

- To love more.
- To love those who mean the most. Every life you touch will touch you back.
- To treasure every enjoyable sensation one has.
- To seek beauty in all its forms.
- To have fun or enjoy life.
- To seek pleasure and avoid pain.
- To be compassionate.
- To be moved by the tears and pain of others, and try to help them out of love and compassion.
- To love others as best we possibly can.
- To eat, drink, and be merry.

To have power, to be better:

- To strive for power and superiority.
- To rule the world.
- To know and master the world.
- To know and master nature.

Life has no meaning:

- Life or human existence has no real meaning or purpose because human existence occurred out of a random chance in nature, and anything that exists by chance has no intended purpose.
- Life has no meaning, but as humans we try to associate a meaning or purpose so we can justify our existence.
- There is no point in life, and that is exactly what makes it so special.

One should not seek to know and understand the meaning of life:

- The answer to the meaning of life is too profound to be known and understood.
- You will never live if you are looking for the meaning of life.
- The meaning of life is to forget about the search for the meaning of life.
- Ultimately, man should not ask what the meaning of his life is, but rather must recognize that it is he who is asked. In a word, each man is questioned by life; and he can only answer to life by answering for his own life; to life he can only respond by being responsible.

Life is bad:

- Life is a bitch, and then you die.
- Better never to have been.